WHO AM I?
AND HOW DID I GET THIS WAY?

**Letting go of the past,
Escaping the limiting triad
Free of limiting Core Beliefs**

By

Joseph E. Spear, D. O.
and
Cecelia A. Spear, M.A

ISBN: 0-75967-615-1 (Electronic)
ISBN: 0-75967-616-X (Softcover))

This book is printed on acid free paper.

Suite 10, 217 Escondido Avenue, Vista, CA 92084

Cover Illustration by Marie Hines
Jspeardo@aol.com
http://doctor.medscape.com/JosephSpearDO

1stBooks – rev. 07/19/02

Purpose

To Help Many More People
Help Many More People
More Effectively.

While this book is basically written for the general public, it is also written as general information for the professional.

Table of Contents

Chapter Five

Chapter Six

Chapter Seven

Chapter Twelve

Chapter Thirteen

Chapter Fourteen

Chapter Fifteen

Acknowledgements

This book could not have been written if it were not for the many individuals who came to us for help in changing their thinking and their lives.

When you work with Core Beliefs, rather than by a diagnostic label, each individual is also a fountain of research information. As we worked with more than 3500 individuals over the years, each one showed us their particular combination of Core Beliefs and how each Core Belief was affecting their lives. Consequently, as each individual taught us his or her unique combination and application of various Core Beliefs, it enabled us to be more efficient and effective with the next individual who had the same Core Beliefs.

A special thanks to Dan Conway who "pushed and pushed" and who patiently read and corrected the punctuation and grammar of this book and earlier papers that were previously published. Don Hanley, Ph.D. for his valuable suggestions and Dr. Marcia Cohen who insisted this material be published. And a very special thanks to Bahbe Majeski, MSC, CHT, Paul Kaprowski, MSW and Debbie Heard.

Introduction

What Happened to Us As We Were Growing Up?

While some readers may discover that they make major changes in their lives simply by reading this book, it is not intended as a workbook leading to freedom from the teachings of childhood. Rather it is to help the reader become more aware of truly basic causes. These basic causes determine the patterns we encounter in our lives.

It is designed to give the reader information and insight as to what may have happened to them while they were growing up. How they have been defining themselves and a general guideline to re-define themselves.

This book may seem like an attack on parents – it is not. It is based on the way we perceive and remember our parents while we are growing up and developing. As you will read in more detail in Chapter 2, we store away reference memories and it is these memories that are consciously and unconsciously used to "prove" our Core Beliefs. Core Beliefs are strongly held opinions that function much like a line of code in a computer. The computer will always function according to that line of code. When the line of code is modified, the computer will always operate the new way.

This material may be quite disturbing as you read certain passages. If so, make a note as to where in the book you became upset and then go to the end of any chapter entitled "Handling Uncomfortable Feelings." This will give you some guidance on handling what you are feeling. "Uncomfortable Feelings" guidance is given at the end of each chapter from Chapter One through Chapter Five. Some individuals may find that it is quite easy for them to understand what the book is saying, until they get to a certain chapter. Trying to read that chapter results in difficulty concentrating or the material seems confusing or they get bored, etc. Most commonly, this indicates a very basic problem area of limiting Core Beliefs for that individual. When you have completed the book, any paragraphs or sections you have noted, will give you additional insight as to what is limiting you.

The authors have often joked about the need for each child to be born with a "how to" book about raising children. Actually, such a book should be distributed before the mother-to-be becomes pregnant and the fathers "are in waiting." Few of us are aware as to how important the mother's attitudes and emotions are to the child's development while in the womb and how the father can affect the unborn child through the mother. Yet far reaching consequences can have their origin here rather than being "genetic."

Basic parental behavior in manipulating and controlling the child as s/he develops may result in great good or great harm. Growing up with a parent who manipulates the child by using double binds has been suggested as a cause of schizophrenia. It certainly is a strong contributor to "neurotic" thinking and behavior.[1]

Fortunately, raising a child by showing the child physical and emotional love, encouraging the child to be all s/he chooses to be, is a powerful force enabling the child to grow up healthy and happy and being all that s/he can be—activating his/her potential—expressing his/her entelechy.[1] Unfortunately the parents referred to in this book, as

---

[1] Expressing your entelechy means to express the highest and finest within you. Every living creature is internally driven to express its full entelechy.

perceived and remembered by the child, seem to be unaware, uncaring or so focused on themselves that the child may feel like nothing more than an object. It is often a case of "victims raising victims raising victims." The parents themselves often regretting their childhood and the way they were raised.

"Since the 1950's, we've seen about a 300% increase in suicide among 15- to 19-year olds. There is about a 90% fatality rate if an adolescent tries to commit suicide with a firearm. If they take an overdose, there's a good chance we can save them."[2]

"A 1995 National Youth Risk Behavior Survey showed that nearly a quarter of students in grades 7 through 12 had seriously considered suicide within the last 12 months of the survey. Nine percent actually attempted suicide and 18% said they had made a specific plan."[3]

Note also the spate of children who killed or planned to kill schoolmates, teachers and others that have come to light just since 1999.

If you were raised in circumstances similar to what is described in this book, you will immediately understand the true source of such desperation in our children.

The names, initials and other identification of actual patients are, of course, fictitious. Too, some case histories are combinations of more than one individual in order to further disguise their identity.

A word about working from Core Beliefs rather than by diagnosis. A diagnosis is a label given to a set of symptoms. The diagnostic label is used as a kind of shorthand so that whenever it is used, the speaker and the listener knows that it refers to a specific constellation of symptoms. For many

---

[2] AAP Update Teen Suicide Policy, Urging Parents to Remove Guns From Homes. quoting David W. Kaplan, University of Colorado School of Medicine, Reuters April 04, 2000
[3] Ibid

therapists, an automatic decision is made about: Is it treatable? What other symptoms should we look for? What are the complications? What is the accepted treatment? What can I predict is the possible outcomes?" While on the surface this seems quite acceptable, it also is quite limiting.

When both the individual and the therapist know what the individual truly believes, they are both empowered to move into a true correction. Change or eliminate the Core Belief causing the undesirable aspects in your life and your life changes accordingly. These changes usually comes about simply, easily, seamlessly and automatically.

A Core Belief is the actual beliefstructure that is causing the desirable or undesirable effects in the person's life and body. It is an exact statement of what the individual actually believes as compared to what s/he thinks s/he believes.

Life limiting Core Beliefs are often so simplistic that when one pops into mind, the individual cannot believe such ridiculous reasoning has caused s/he life long problems. An example of this is: "Anxiety enables me to feel alive."

Even assuming that a particular diagnosis is correct (one-third are said to be wrong), its application causes both therapist and patient to immediately react accordingly. Often times, after being given a diagnosis, the individual will look it up in an attempt to find out what other symptoms s/he will have and what to expect. While it may seem empowering at first glance, in many instances it is quite limiting. It maybe quite limiting because for that particular individual all the aspects are simply not true for them, there may only one or two. Too, the individual may unconsciously add symptoms s/he did not previously have until s/he read what symptoms were to be expected.

If the mental health practitioner is a psychiatrist, a diagnosis of depression leads the psychiatrist to decide whether it is with anxiety or without anxiety, etc. At that point s/he then chooses a medication accordingly. If the medication causes side effects or doesn't work the psychiatrist must go on to something else.

Usually some other medication.

The authors are not attacking the use of medication in the treatment of psychotics, but the use of a Core Belief approach is much more effective than medication for much of the so-called neuroses. It also has some surprisingly effective results in organic disease.

It has been said that the difference between a neurosis and a psychosis is that the neurotic is nervous about his world and the psychotic creates his own world.

An individual may have the classic signs of depression, and by using a Core Belief approach, we want to know what the individual believes that is causing this kind of response. Careful questioning often reveals that neurotic depression is the defense against strong feelings of anger. The feelings of anger are due to feelings of helplessness following one or more events. The individual has come to believe that it is better to numb themselves rather than have the emotional turmoil engendered by strong feelings of helplessness. Later, when the individual sees his/her life in a shambles, help is sought for the depression. The real problem to be dealt with is the preceding event(s) resulting in the helplessness.

Consider the individual who has a Core Belief that he needs to feel anxiety in order to stay alive, yet seeks to remove the anxious feelings. Let us say it another way: he believes he needs to feel anxiety to know he is alive. He cannot handle feeling that cause anxiety all the time, and looks for an escape. He could use drugs, alcohol, etc., but this individual has some how chosen to use depression. Unfortunately it depresses everything. It does not selectively depress the anxiety feelings, it depresses all of his feelings. If there was a medication that could completely removed his depression, the anxiety would return in some way and have to be dealt with, since it disrupts his life.

Thus the authors' form of facilitation is not pharmaceutical, but a gentle search into when the depression began, what was the individual feeling helpless about in that situation, or combination of situations, and achieving resolution. We do not see ourselves as "therapists," but rather Entelechists. An Entelechist is one who helps another facilitate activating more of his or her potential and in turn expressing more of his or her entelechy.

Your entelechy is the highest and finest within you. Each of us has a built in drive to express that entelechy at its fullest.

When both the individual and the Entelechist understand the Core Beliefs causing the undesirable symptoms or life pattern, it is usually a simple matter to shift out of it. This is because we never mess up our lives with nice, logical Core Beliefs structured with adult logic. In the authors' experience, it is always the Core Beliefs structured during childhood and carried over into adulthood that are most often the true cause of the problem. The "child within" is dead and gone, but the adult has inherited the beliefs of "child-it-was."

An interesting exception to this is the woman who had mild to moderate depression for years. She was one of the very few cases whose depressive symptoms did not follow the above pattern. We found out that as a 9 year old child, she came home from school one day and told her mother she was "depressed." Her mother immediately responded by hugging her, telling her she loved the child and other verbal feelings of love. She then took the 9-year old out to a movie and dinner and they had a great time. The Core Belief: "The way to get love is to be depressed."

Core Beliefs vs. Personality Types

Classifying individuals by personality types is not very empowering. Simply classifying an individual as a "Type A" personality, and listing the differences between that and a "Type B," does not give any information as to what is causing the individual to be that way. Clinical evidence indicates that each characteristic of one's personality is determined by one or more Core Beliefs. Consequently, when working with Core Beliefs it is possible to achieve changes in personality by accessing and changing the operant Core Beliefs. What the authors think happens is that the individual becomes the personality s/he really is. The personality traits that would have been apparent, if they had not taken on certain limiting Core Beliefs.

We've been asked if nearly all of the societal problems are rooted in narcissistic parenting and the double bind. We certainly encounter this in people with:

> No inner sense as to who they really are
> Deep fears
> Powerful needs to be in control
> Difficulty expressing themselves
> Stunted emotional development
> Criminal behavior
> A need to manipulate, lie, cheat, deceive, etc.

Probably not every one exhibiting such behavior, but many, many individuals. Just growing up in an environment of emotional deprivation can result in any of the above.

Importance of Uncomfortable Feelings

It is common for people reading this material to find that certain uncomfortable feelings begin to come up. If this happens to you, you have probably been taught during your childhood to stifle your feelings, to do whatever is required so you do not express them or feel them.

This is absolutely the poorest way to handle your feelings.

Suppressed or denied feelings often lead to physical disorders.

At the end of many of the chapters is a section entitled Handling Uncomfortable Feelings. Such uncomfortable feelings may be: guilt, anger, fear, sadness, etc.

If you find by the end of a particular chapter that you have a strong, uncomfortable feeling arising, it will be of great value to you to follow the guidelines of this section and allow such feelings to pass through you. Should such feelings come up while reading a particular chapter, it is of value to stop and allow yourself to feel and let such feelings pass through you at that time.

It is important to allow yourself to do this until you discover the uncomfortable feelings are no longer there, or you have fallen asleep, or you connect with the original event (the reference memory) that these feelings are coming from. In which case, write down a description of this event. Almost always such feelings are part of a memory rather than something in the present.

Re-Defining Your Self

To "define" means: to trace the precise outlines of; to determine or state the extent and nature of; to give the distinguishing characteristics of; to state the meanings of; to designate."

We define our selves by our Core Beliefs. What we really believe about ourselves, our bodies, our world, etc. Our core beliefs define all that. Our Core Beliefs are like a set of automatic decisions that we have incorporated over the years.

We originally take them on in the form of

- rules: "In order to stay alive I must feel angry and sad."
- safe guards: "I can only be safe if no one sees me."
- personal superstitions (A personal superstition is a belief taken on by the child that seems to be true, but to the adult is almost nonsense): "If I am mad, no one can hurt me." Or,
- short cuts to understanding and dealing with life and ourselves: "You can't trust men."

Thus they define our extent and our nature.

A few examples of some other Core Beliefs are:

"I am not worthy of being happy."

"Because my mother got pregnant with me before she was married, I am bad."

"If I am happy, I will be alone and have to take care of myself."

"All the men in the Smith family go bald and since I am a man in the Smith family I, too, will lose my hair."

"Independence means you have to be alone."

"If I forgive someone it means they were right and I was wrong."

And there are many, many more. To date we have cataloged over 600 beliefs that are life limiting.

These Core Beliefs are strongly held beliefs that range from being completely true and valid, to being totally false and incorrect. However, like a computer following a line of code, we follow each and every one of them because we believe each one to be completely true.

We go into a kind of trance state when any of these automatic decisions becomes active.

If the active Core Belief is life enhancing, we do not give it another thought. If it is life limiting, it becomes an arena of struggle and dissatisfaction. Too, you may feel helpless to change it or that you have no control over it.

Thus we define who and what we are: our thoughts, feelings, actions and reactions – by these Core Beliefs.

What our Core Beliefs say about our selves – defines our-selves:

As to how we think and feel about ourselves.

As to what we think others think and feel about us.

As to how the various organs and tissues of our body function – its state of health or disease.

As to our arenas of abilities and faults

success and failure;
love and money.
power and helplessness,
struggle and pressure,
acceptance and rage,
God and guilt,
forgiveness and hate, etc.

As to our parents and how we raise our children.

All this and more is how we define ourselves by means of what we <u>really</u> believe—our Core Beliefs!

Thus, the way to upgrade, change, eliminate, "shift gears out of" the undesirable aspects of our thinking and our behavior; the undesirable patterns in our lives; is to re-define ourselves.

Re-defining means to change our Core Beliefs so that we "shift gears" into being, thinking and feeling the way we want to be – to re-define our Core Beliefs, re-state them as new, upgraded, more life enhancing definitions. Thus re-structuring our automatic decisions.

And as we re-define our Core Beliefs, we re-define ourselves.

As we re-define ourselves, the various aspects of our bodies, our minds and our spirits shift into line with the new definitions of self.

The reader should not lose hope. Every one of the limiting Core. Beliefs and conditions described in this book is correctable.

Sometimes just getting information about certain patterns and beliefs is enough to shift you out of it and into a new definition of yourself in that particular area.

Other times a skilled facilitator is required to help guide you through it. We call such a facilitator an "Entelechist." An Entelechist is one who helps you to realize more of your entelechy. Your entelechy is the expression of the highest and finest within you. All conscious entities have the inner drive to reach and express their entelechy. Another way of expressing this is that to activate your entelechy completely is to use all of your potential.

None of the circumstances, conditions, Core Beliefs, etc., described herein are simply genetic or chemical. Every one is due to the thought processes of our minds. Please note that we said "mind" not "brain."

Consider the brain as a TV set. It receives and translate energy coming into it into sounds and pictures.

Consider the mind as the source of the energy which is processed by the brain – the transmitter signals beamed at the TV set.

Chapter One

The Limiting Triad and Lizzie Borden Rage

"The former sailor suspected of killing prostitutes in ports around the world was abused by his father and traumatized by the death of an infant brother, his family says. Relatives find it difficult to imagine how a quiet child who earned decent grades, played Nintendo and enjoyed fishing and baseball could emerge as a suspected serial killer. "The Eric we raised could not have done these things...This is just not the person we know...We just did the best we could...We're having a real problem reconciling all of this." [4]

Limiting Triad

The Limiting Triad is like a three-legged stool. Each leg represents one of the following and how it affects the young, developing child:

Leg One: Narcissistic (highly self centered) Parents

Leg Two: Putting the child into Double Binds where s/he is given two conflicting commands and is expected to fulfill both and from which the child has no escape.

Leg Three: Circumstances flooding the child with certain emotions that the child continues to maintain into

---

[4] *North County Times*, "The Back Page," Vista, CA, April 17, 2000

adulthood. The child has come to believe these emotions are necessary for survival.

a. O'Henry Effect Episode or Sudden Traumatic Emotional Reversal (STER). A disastrous event which results in the child blaming joy, curiosity, etc. for causing the disaster and vows never to let those feelings occur again. Even though what the child blames as the cause had no part in causing the disaster.

b. Uncomfortable emotions experienced while in the womb or around the time of birth and incorporated as being necessary for life.

The effect of any one or more of these three is to communicate to the child that s/he cannot be who and what s/he really is. This is devastating to the child and engenders great problems in childhood and adult life.

When Alice Miller is speaking of the child who grows up in an atmosphere of double binds, what she quotes applies to the effects of any one of the three "legs" of the triad:

"The true self has been in 'a state of non-communication,…because it had to be protected.' The patient never needs to hide anything else so thoroughly, so deeply, and for so long a time as he has hidden his true self. Thus it is like a miracle each time to see how much individuality has survived behind such dissimulation, denial and self-alienation, and can reappear…"[5]

The repression of the "real self" being enforced by two factors:

1. the parental figure(s), and the[6]

---

[5] *The Drama of the Gifted Child*, Alice Miller, Basic Books Inc., NY, NY, 1981, page 20

[6] A parental figure is usually the actual parent – mother or father.

2. survival need of the child – the child must act to protect itself, Thus it makes a decision (Autonomy) to do whatever it takes to survive and avoid pain, if possible. Remember, to the child, it all boils down to survival! Staying alive with as little pain as possible.

A feeling of helplessness develops – and grows in a bed of silent desperation.

Individuals have pointed out in therapy that such feelings were present even as toddlers. With this feeling of helplessness comes the natural application of anger to overcome the horrible feelings of helplessness. With anger failing to get resolution comes the anesthetic we call "depression." For in such cases, the child is not allowed to express such anger. In fact, it is often denied the right to even feel anger. For that is not allowed by the parental figure(s).

Event(s) Helplessness Anger Resolution No Resolution Depression often with later Physical Symptoms developing.

Lizzie Borden Rage

"Lizzie Borden took an axe and gave her mother 40 whacks, when she saw what she had done, she gave her father 41."[7]

However there are those instances in which one or more other adults are experienced by the child as being a kind of parent, such as a guardian. These others are "parental figures" and usually have the same power over the child as the biological parent. A terrifying sibling may also have the same effect.

[7] It should be noted here that Lizzie Borden was found not guilty of those murders. Reference here and elsewhere is simply meant to demonstrate the rage that can develop towards parents during childhood.

Anger is usually a spontaneous emotional attempt to achieve some kind of communication and understanding. The failure of such an attempt and the ongoing sense of helplessness results in rage. An angry response is, "How come you did that?!" or, "How come you didn't do that?!" or, "How come you treat me this way?!" It, and the hormones released, are meant to bring about physical action of some kind. On Core Belief levels it is an automatic response meant to overcome the sense of helplessness the individual is feeling and to convert it into resolution. The longer the child is stifled and restricted from expressing its true feelings, thoughts and desires, the stronger the sense of anger becomes. If the expression of the anger is not allowed, ignored or otherwise ineffective, it increases in strength and severity. And so the anger – a feeling of displeasure with a desire to fight back – eventually becomes a furious, forceful, violent, multi-level ongoing emotion. We call this emotion: "rage."

Let us pause here for a moment.

It is important to realize that we are not actually attacking the parental figures, we are dealing with the memories of the child.

The fact that the child, now an adult, remembers the parental figures in a certain way does not prove that is the way the parental figures actually were. It is the child's perception of such individuals. Even when, as an adult, the individual has come to terms with the parental figure, there may still be the active Core Beliefs put in place during childhood. And so the child, now an adult, frequently experiences mixed emotions concerning that parent.

As with any emotion, this ever increasing anger, this rage, must be expressed somehow. Our emotions are meant to be felt.

They are meant to be expressed through the various body parts and completely released as they arise. When the expression of such feelings is not allowed, regardless of the age of the individual, the functioning of our bodies, minds and spirits is progressively disturbed.

The child, growing up in an atmosphere that restricts what s/he can do, be, have and feel, first develops a sense of helplessness, followed by anger, followed by the "anesthetic" called "depression." This "anesthetic" is an important defense mechanism in that it helps control the anger and rage by shifting into a kind of numbness. In a sense this is easier on mental and physiological functions as compared to being in a constant state of anger.

Consequently, the authors never "attack" the depression, but seek to find the origin of the need for such a defense. In some cases, it may begin in the womb where the child may have "absorbed" the mother's feelings.

The longer restrictions are in place, the more helpless the child feels, the greater the anger becomes, until it turns into a smoldering rage. The extreme outcome of loss of control of this internalized rage is to turn it on parental figures (or those who symbolize the parental figures) violently.

Fortunately most of these children do not lose control. They develop a multi-level "tension" to keep it under control. At times it spills out in various disguises.

Controlling the Rage to Kill

"Teens Who Cut Selves On the Rise: In what appears to be a disturbing national trend...many local school and family counselors are reporting a rise in the number of teenagers-mostly girls- who are

mutilating themselves to relieve pressure they are feeling from friends and at home and school."[8]

They often withdraw. They may turn the anger on themselves by becoming accident-prone or repeatedly damaging their bodies in various ways such as cutting themselves with razor blades; they may set fires, be cruel to animals, wet the bed even as adolescents, bully other children, become anorexic or bulimic, etc. Often such children will develop an ongoing, internal "preparedness." They take on the personal myth or superstition that if they stay alert, on guard, tense, do not relax nor become calm, peaceful, etc. that this will keep them alive.[9]

"My tension keeps me together!"

Why is this a myth or superstition? Because at the time of its origin it was the only solution the child could come up with. And it is almost always incorrect! It is "proven" to be accurate because the child is now an adult and still alive. Often, such preparedness had nothing to do with the child's survival, it only seemed so.

Once upon a time a young man who had never been out of the city decided to see what the rural area looked like. As he drove along the various roads and lanes, he noticed there was always a box attached to a post at the driveway of each farm. On the box was a little red flag that could be raised up or down. He had no idea as to what the contraption was, but every farm had one. Coming upon a farmer standing beside one, he pulled up and asked the farmer what the box was for. The farmer decided to play a joke on this city boy and replied: "Well, it is to keep the tigers away." The young

---

[8] The Vista *North County Times*, "Front Page," Sunday, April 30, 2000

[9] The presence of these first three is used to evaluate potential violence. It is inadequate

man was astonished. "There are no tigers around here!" The farmer said, "See, its working!!"

So it is with the child's myth about having to stay so tense and limited. There are rare occasions where a parental figure was truly life threatening to the child, but more often what truly kept the parental figure from killing the child was that the parental figure chose not to. Because the parental figure never had any intention of abandoning or killing the child.

The ultimate solution is to so bury the rage that, even on some sub-conscious levels, the individual is not aware of its presence and influence. For, to the child, to release the tension means to release the rage and someone will die. That "tension" will stay in place for life, unless the child, now an adult, realizes it is no longer needed. That s/he is not now a trapped child. That s/he has choices and among those choices is the choice to forgive. In such a case, forgiveness – letting go, is a very powerful prerequisite to allowing oneself to utilize one's potential and realize one's entelechy. More about forgiving in Chapter Ten.[10]

It is common to so strictly limit one's self for two reasons:

1. To keep from being attacked and damaged by the parental figure.
2. To keep one's self from attacking and damaging the parental figure.

Consequently, the therapeutic approach that grew out of all this is called "Entelechial Therapy." The process is called "PReP." PReP is the Potential Releasing Process. It is describe in more detail in Appendix I.

---

[10] Realizing your entelechy is realizing the full activation and expression of your potential.

Effects of the Limiting Triad

(Triad = Very Self Centered Parents, Double Bind, The Need for Miserable Feelings)

If you grew up experiencing one or more "legs" of the Limiting Triad:

- it is not permissible for you to be who and what you really are.
- It is not permissible for you to have your own feelings and have them respected.
- It is not permissible for you to have your own desires and strive to fulfill them.
- It is not permissible for you to have your own personality.
- It is not permissible for you to do what you want to do.
- It is not permissible for you to enjoy what you want to enjoy.
- It is not permissible for you to be happy.
- It is not permissible for you to be calm and peaceful

The "you" that you are, the real you, must be kept hidden.

Then you act out the role dictated by the parental figure. This is almost always the dominant parental figure.

If you are a child growing up in an atmosphere of narcissistic parenting and double binds, what is permissible is for you to be:

"The way I want you to be, think, feel and act. Even though the verbal and non-verbal commands I give you may be impossible to do, you are to do them any way."

The narcissistic parent communicates both verbally and non-verbally to the child not only what is expected, but demanded, and often violently enforced. In every instance it will be limitation and acting a role. Being unreal. And if that limitation is not obeyed, it will be met with pain-inflicting actions – if not physically, definitely emotionally.

The child raised in Double Binds is "between a rock and a hard place." "Damned if I do and damned if I don't."

Where the adult can refuse to follow either or both of conflicting orders, the child is trapped. S/he needs the parental figure to supply the necessities of life. The child is well aware that if the parental figure chooses not to do so, the child will die.

Not only are those things which maintain physical survival important, but the child, on some level knows it also needs the physical expressions of love: being hugged, kissed, appreciated and told it is loved, special, cared about.

The child needs to be allowed to be curious, happy, active, eager, trusted, praised, seen, heard and gently guided as it expresses and lives in its own unique way. It needs to feel cared about for who and what the child really is rather than forcibly pressed into a mold. It is not uncommon for the adult who grew up in any one, or combination, of the legs of the Triad to symbolically see itself as wrapped in chains or as an Egyptian mummy.

Consequently the child goes to great effort to try to fulfill the demands placed on it. Remember, to the child, rejection means death. This is because the child, in its simplistic reasoning, believes that it will not survive if rejected by the dominant parent. If rejected, there is no other way for the child to get what it needs to live. The child is well aware someone else must so provide. Obviously the dominant parent is the boss and everyone else follows that parent's orders.

Double Binds force the child into great anxiety and have been blamed for causing psychosis such as schizophrenia.[11]

---

[11] *The Double Bind*, Sluzki and Ransom, Editors, Grune & Stratton., NY, NY, 1976

While current thinking tends to discredit this, double binds are quite obviously creators of neurotic behavior.

The authors have never encountered an individual raised by a narcissistic parent who was not also put in double binds:

"You can be anything you want to be, my son…as long as I approve."

"It is important that you show you love me, but don't touch me."

Where the O'Henry Effect (Sudden Traumatic Emotional Reversal) has occurred, the child is so shocked, startled and frightened, that s/he blames the emotions immediately preceding the trauma as the cause of the trauma. Since such emotions are usually those of joy, happiness, pleasure, curiosity, etc. s/he takes on that such emotions and behavior are:

1. not permissible
2. potentially fatal

This will be discussed in detail in Chapter Five: The O'Henry Effect.

Personal Law of Survival

For many people, out of all this comes a Personal Law of Survival. A Personal Law of Survival is a Core Belief that the individual puts together which is designed to help him or her survive not only in the environments previously described as the Triad, but for the rest of his or her life.

Unfortunately, this Personal Law of Survival is put together by a young, naïve, terrified, child who because of its dependency, not only feels helpless but has a slowly growing anger. Because it is designed to help one stay alive, it influences every aspect of life.

10

We will go into this in more detail in Chapter Nine: Personal Law of Survival.

Do You Have One or More of the Triad?

Questions to help you decide:

1. Who was the boss in the family? Mother? Father? Grandparent? Sibling? Other?
2. Was it unsafe to reveal your true feelings to the dominant person in the family?
3. Was it unsafe to ask for what you really wanted to the dominant person in the family?
4. Was it easy to feel guilty at times, even though you were not the guilty person?
5. Was the dominant person in the family physically and or emotional unaffectionate and distant towards you?
6. Was the dominant person in the family self centered to the extent that you had to be the person she or he wanted you to be (or at least highly controlling)?

There are three basic kinds of self-centered people (narcissistic):

If one or more people that you lived with treated you this way, please put a checkmark in box a., b., and/or c.1. or c.2. It is important to be aware that not only can mothers act like this, but fathers, other parental figures, siblings and the family clan itself may treat the child this way.

a. Stage Mother: wants the child to succeed so she feels like a success
b. Queen: teaches the child that he or she is only there to take care of the parent's wants and needs.
c. Attacker:

1) Direct: criticizes or insults the child any time the child excels.
2) Indirect: ignores or sabotages the child's successes.

7. As a child growing up, were you put "between a rock and a hard place"? Given conflicting messages or orders that you were to follow even though it was impossible to do both?

   EX: "Johnny you can be anything you want to be as long as your father and I approve of it."

8. As a child, were there times you felt invisible or wished you were invisible so others wouldn't mistreat you or expect much from you?
9. As a child, and perhaps even now, a sense that you don't know your true identity?
10. In your relationships do they eventually fall apart or turn out to be quite disappointing even though you thought it would not happen this time?
11. In your career does it seem that about the time you start to reach some level of improvement or success something happens and you start all over again?
12. Were you an unwanted child when your parents found out your mother was pregnant?
13. Were you not the girl or boy the dominant parent wanted (the "wrong" sex)?
14. Was labor induced (started by injections or some medical procedure or trauma)?
15. If you were a Cesarean Section, had contractions started on their own before you were taken from the womb?
16. Was your mother basically unhappy during the pregnancy?
17. Were there any problems at the time of your delivery?

18. Does it seem like you have difficulty making decisions on your own?
19. Do you tend to do nothing unless pushed into it by someone else?
20. Do you find that you can't accomplish your own goals, but have no trouble accomplishing the goals set by others?
21. Do you tend to avoid doing things that attracts the attention of others?
22. Do you get nervous when you find yourself being really happy?
23. Have you noticed that you always have some kind of a problem going on; when one clears up there is another one arising?
24. Did you believe as a child that others did not listen or hear you?
25. Do you find you avoid completing things?
26. Do you feel unworthy, undeserving of getting the things you want?
27. Do you have, or have you had, conditions such as Chronic Fatigue Syndrome, Hypoglycemia, or the use of drugs that periodically cause you to do poorly or become non-functional?
28. When you were growing up, was there a big problem or near disaster you caused or thought you caused?
29. Does it seem like the harder you work for something, the more likely you are not to get it, or that everything seems to be a struggle?
30. Is there a "miserable feeling" or combination of "miserable feelings" that keep coming up in your life on a fairly regular basis?
31. Is it a little scary to think about being completely on your own; no one waiting in the wings to consult with, help you or be with you in some way?
32. Have there been extended periods during which you were uncomfortable being alone when you were not

particularly involved with or communicating with someone on a day to day basis?

33. Does it seem like you have to maintain a pretty tight control on your anger much of the time?

34. Does it seem like you are always holding some kind of tension much of the time? If yes, any particular parts of your body?_____

35. Does your life seem to be one of living under pressure or always having to struggle?

Interpreting Your Answers

Emotional Deprivation and/or Abuse:

If you grew up in an atmosphere of Emotional Deprivation and or Abuse you probably answered the following questions as "Yes":

1. Was it unsafe to reveal your true feelings to the dominant person in the family?

2. Was it unsafe to ask for what you really wanted to the dominant person in the family?

3. Was it easy to feel guilty at times, even though you were not the guilty person?

4. Was the dominant person in the family physically and or emotionally unaffectionate and distant towards you?

5. Was the dominant person in the family self centered to the extent that you had to be the person she or he wanted you to be (or at least highly controlling)?

Narcissistic Parenting

If you grew up under the control of a narcissistic parent or parental figure you probably answered the following questions "Yes":

All of the above, plus checking one or more of the following:

a. Stage Mother: wants the child to succeed so she feels like a success
b. Queen: teaches the child that he or she is only there to take care of the parent's wants and needs.
c. Attacker:

1) Direct: criticizes or insults the child any time the child excels.
2) Indirect: ignores or sabotages the child's successes.

Double Binds

If you grew up under the control of a parent or parental figure who subjected you to Double Binds, you probably checked many of the above, plus:

1. As a child growing up were you put "between a rock and a hard place." Given conflicting messages or orders that you were to follow even though it was impossible to do both? EX: "Johnny you can be anything you want to be – as long as your father and I approve of it."

Peri-Natal[12]

If you had the Belief that you must feel and experience certain feelings which came from the peri-natal period you probably checked:

1. Were you an unwanted child when your parents found out your mother was pregnant?
2. Were you not the girl or boy the dominant parent wanted (the "wrong" sex)?

---

[12] Peri-natal: that period from conception to shortly after birth as compared to "Pre-natal"- before birth only.

3. Was labor induced (started by injections or some medical procedure or trauma)?
4. If you were a Cesarean Section, had contractions started on their own before you were taken from the womb?
5. Was your mother basically unhappy during the pregnancy?
6. Were there any problems at the time of your delivery?
7. Is there a "miserable feeling," or combination of "miserable feelings," that keep coming up in your life on a fairly regular basis?

Lizzie Borden Rage

If you checked the following, you probably have some degree of "Lizzie Borden Rage":

1. Does it seem like you have to maintain a pretty tight control on your anger much of the time?
2. Does it seem like you are always holding some kind of tension much of the time? If yes, any particular parts of your body?_____

Other Evidence of Growing Up in the Triad

If you answered the following questions "Yes" they are additional evidence of one or more of the Triad:

1. As a child, were there times you felt invisible, or wished you were invisible, so others wouldn't mistreat you or expect much from you?
2. As a child and, perhaps even now, a sense that you don't know your true identity?
3. In your relationships do they eventually fall apart or turn out to be quiet disappointing even though you thought it would not happen this time?
4. In your career does it seem like about the time you start to reach some level of improvement or success something happens and you start all over again?

5. Does it seem like you have difficulty making decisions on your own?
6. Do you tend to do nothing unless pushed into it by someone else?
7. Do you find that you can't accomplish your own goals, but have no trouble accomplishing the goals set by others?
8. Do you tend to avoid doing things that attracts the attention of others
9. Do you get nervous when you find yourself being really happy?
10. Have you noticed that you always have some kind of a problem going on; when one clears up there is another one arising?
11. Did you believe as a child that others did not listen or hear you?
12. Do you find you avoid completing things?
13. Do you feel unworthy, undeserving of getting the things you want?
14. Do you have or have you had conditions such as Chronic Fatigue Syndrome, Hypoglycemia or the use of drugs that periodically cause you to do poorly or become non-functional?

Sudden Traumatic Emotional Reversal—STER

If you experienced an O'Henry Event—Sudden Traumatic Emotional Reversal, you probably also checked:

1. When you were growing up, was there a big problem or near disaster you caused or thought you caused?

Survival Dependency

If you have taken on some degree of Survival Dependency you probably checked:

1. Does it seem like the harder you work for something, the more likely you are not to get it, or that every thing seems a struggle?
2. Is it a little scary to think about being completely on your own; no one waiting in the wings to consult with, help you or be with you in some way?
3. Have there been extended periods during which you were uncomfortable being alone– when you were not particularly involved with, or communicating with, someone on a day today basis?

Need to Struggle or Be Under Pressure

This is often indicated when you check:

1. Does it seem like the harder you work for something, the more likely you are not to get it or that every thing seems a struggle?
2. Does your life seem to be one of living under pressure or always having to struggle?

Summary of Your Findings:

Emotional Deprivation and/or Abuse
Narcissistic Parenting
Double Bind Peri-Natal
Sudden Traumatic Emotional Reversal
Survival Dependency
Signs of Lizzie Borden Rage
Struggle/Pressure

Check out what you are feeling right now. Perhaps it is of value to go to the end of this chapter on Handling Uncomfortable Feelings and do that for a while. Then come back and go on with your reading.

It is not uncommon for an individual to have checked many of the boxes, since these feelings and circumstances are often found in place during their growth and development period.

It is rare for the child to grow up in an environment where there is just Emotional Deprivation and Abuse. This is because these experiences are usually a part of each of the three legs of the Triad.

Survival Dependency may occur as the result of the child coming to believe that s/he does not make good decisions and Thus retreats into a set of Core Beliefs that the safest way to stay alive is to have someone else always there to rely on. This other person becomes a rescuer/caretaker, and is expected to at least help make decisions.

While Sudden Traumatic Emotional Reversal may be the result of a completely accidental event, it is often encountered when a parental figure unexpectedly lashes out at the child.

And, of course, you can not go through a childhood encompassing any of the above with out developing feelings of helplessness and the attempt to compensate via anger.

While not an absolute, your answers to these questions should lead you to examine your memories of your childhood teachings carefully. Please understand <u>we are not attacking your parents</u>. We are not interested in the way the parental figures actually were in your life back then. <u>What we are interested in, is the way you perceived them and stored them as memories</u>.

At this point, all is memory and it is important to realize that:

- The younger you are when you store a memory, the more distorted it is.
- The more upset you are at the time of storing a memory, the more distorted it is.
- If you are both young and upset at the time, the memory is really distorted, especially as to its interpretation.

Nevertheless, we react to all our memories as though they are 100% accurate. The key to all this is your memory of the relationship with the Dominant Parent while growing up, and the events held in your mind about this parent.

Handling Uncomfortable Feelings

Your feelings are naturally designed to flow through you.

Your feelings and your emotional state are naturally designed to be:

1. Physically experienced, and
2. Consciously acted upon

All your feelings are naturally designed to help. No feeling is a negative feeling or harmful feeling, because each feeling is naturally designed to be experienced. You just allow it to be.

You just allow the feeling/emotion to flow into whatever feelings/emotions it is going to go through: a series of changes until you feel empty, drained or comfortable again.

You will discover that it leaves you feeling better.

Suppose you are feeling guilty. You simply say to your self:

"I am feeling what I think is (state the feeling)…I feel this uncomfortable feeling…in my (state whatever parts of your body you are feeling it in…)…just because I am feeling this way does not mean that it is true…or false…it is just a feeling I am having…and I am just allowing myself to feel this way for now"…Perhaps after a few minutes…you discover that this uncomfortable feeling has changed…and now it feels like another uncomfortable feeling…again you say: "I am feeling what I think is (state the feeling)…I feel this uncomfortable feeling in my (state parts of body)…just because I am feeling this way does not make it true…or false…it is just an uncomfortable feeling I am having about something and I am allowing myself to feel this way for now"…Perhaps after a few minutes the feeling changes again and you say to yourself…"I am feeling what I think is (state feeling)…I feel this uncomfortable feeling in my (state body parts)…just because I feel this way doesn't mean it is true or false…it is just an uncomfortable feeling I am having about something…and I am just allowing myself to feel this way for now"…Keep doing this until you find the uncomfortable feelings have gone and the feeling you are left with is comfortable or at least neutral.

If it leads you to an early event in your life—then that will be the true source of the uncomfortable feelings you are having at the time. Write them down. Somehow they will be related to the problems going on in your life now.

Joseph E. Spear, D.O., Cecelia Ann Spear, M.A.

Chapter Two

Personal Reality and Core Beliefs[13]

Probably the most comprehensive material on the effects of deeply held (Core) Beliefs on every aspect of our lives is found in *The Nature of Personal Reality* by Jane Roberts.[14] In 1969, we were greatly dissatisfied with the available psychiatric, psychological and counseling approaches available. This concept of Core Beliefs held promise of a simple, effective approach to emotional and physical problems. It was very simple to apply and welcomed by our patients. We soon found that the use of the Core Belief concept was simple, easy and highly effective. It was simpler and more empowering because it focused on the true causative factors – the active Core Beliefs. It soon became obvious that treating a diagnosis or a "personality type" was like digging for clams a mile inland. The Core Beliefs put you right in the middle of the clam bed.

A Core Belief approach is able to help people much more specifically and accurately, because the *Core Belief is the cause of the proble*m. The Core Belief defines the thoughts, feelings, attitudes, concepts, ideas, actions and reactions of the individual.

It is a powerful influence on the physical body and its functioning, down to the individual cells.

---

[13] Published in modified form in *Phyre Talk*, Phoenix Phyre Books, Encinitas, CA 92024

[14] *The Nature of Personal Reality*, Jane Roberts, Prentice-Hall, Inc. Englewood cliff, NJ, 1974

In the New Testament of the Judeo-Christian Bible this is indirectly referred to:

"Train up a child in the way he should go and, when he is old, he will not depart from it."[15]

Unless modified or eliminated, the Core Beliefs that you "train" a child to take on will be with him all the days of his life.

Even those which prevent him from functioning fully and wholly. It is important to remember that the parent may have no idea that s/he is training the child to believe various life limiting Core Beliefs. Often they are simply teaching the child what the parent believes is valid.

Victims raising victims raising victims.

The children of narcissistic parents often become narcissistic themselves. And such "training" is often not done directly, but quite indirectly.

An example of parents indirectly training their children is how the parents behave in resolving their differences. How they argue and go about getting resolution. At the annual meeting of the Association for Advancement of Behavior Therapy, Elizabeth Santa Ana reported:[16]

"It was really incredible how we were able to link parental styles of managing conflict with their teenagers to their teenagers' styles of managing conflicts with their peers, and a whole range of other problems going on in the school."

"If a parent was authoritarian or permissive, the child tended to be coercive when attempting to resolve a conflict, whether with parents or peers. These children also were

---

[15] *Proverbs* Chapter 22:6
[16] *Clinical Psychiatry News* 28(5):42,2000 "Parents' Conflict Resolution Styles Shape Teens," as reported by medscape.com 06/11/2000

likely to engage in fights, more likely to use drugs, and to fail in school; they often had trouble handling problems with teachers."

Another means by which parents unwittingly "train" their children is "modeling" or parental copying. That is, the child tends to copy various behaviors and actions of one or more of the parental figures it lives with. It models its behavior into certain aspects of their likeness.

The child is unable to differentiate what is desirable and what is undesirable in its early stages of this modeling. Later in life, when the child, now an adult, more closely examines its behaviors, traits, etc., it can quite clearly see that it has taken on both.

It is important to realize that each step along the road to adulthood, the child has made conscious decisions and taken on various Core Beliefs. These become automatic decisions and are believed by the developing child to be true, accurate and of great value.

The authors have never worked with an individual who on some level did not know why s/he took on a particular Core Belief.

The Core Belief is always rooted in a reference memory. It is not uncommon for individuals who have been copying highly undesirable aspects of a parental figure to say, "I took that on because I didn't know any other way to be. That is how Mom acted and I wanted Dad to love me like he did her."

The child observes and evaluates quite closely and deliberately. It knows that it is wholly dependent on those in charge of it – the parental figures. And of the parental figures the dominate one is the one to be feared, adored, idolized, impressed and motivated to make sure the child has its needs fulfilled. This is covered in more detail in Chapter Ten: Unfinished Business.

From its observations and using a very simplistic, naïve logic, the child comes to various decisions that are deeply integrated and have the same influence on the child as a line of code does on a computer. Therein lies the problem.

The reasoning ability of the naïve, developing child is not sufficient or accurate, in many instances. Particularly in instances where there is great upset. The child simply does not have the skills, experience and knowledge of people, and so makes mal-adaptive decisions which are incorporated as Core Beliefs—automatic decisions.

The child believes its observations, evaluations and reasoning are absolutely correct, and sets up a set of Core Beliefs as automatic decisions about itself, the world and everything in it. The parental figures may be highly intelligent, average or of below average intelligence. They may be very skillful at training the child in their ways. They may be totally unaware of what they are teaching. It makes no difference. It is how the child perceives itself and those around it. It is what the child takes on as to what seems to work to maintain and insure its survival.

Consequently, to the casual observer it may seem that certain Core Beliefs of the child just "seem to happen." Actually, the formation of the Core Belief can often be traced quite clearly and accurately to the event(s) that resulted in its formation, and what the purposes were, in the mind of the child, for taking on such a Core Belief.

Accessing the individual's Core Beliefs in relation to life distorting patterns of thinking and behavior, empower both the individual and those trying to assist him/her.

This, too, is referred to biblically:

"When I was a child, I spake as a child, I understood as a child, I thought as a child: but when I became a man I put away childish things."[17]

Naturally you should have put away those limiting Core Beliefs you took on as a child as you move into adulthood, because such Core Beliefs were designed to help you

---

[17] *I Corinthians*, Chapter 13:11

function as a child in a particular environment and not as an adult. If not put away, they now have you limiting your functioning as an adult.

An easy analogy of a Core Belief is to equate it to a line of code in a computer. The programmer structures and sets in what s/he believes is the best set of instructions for the computer to follow. These instructions are there for the computer which has to always follow them from then on – exactly as structured. They are always meant to accomplish a particular purpose effectively, efficiently and when necessary.

The child is the programmer of its mind.

The child uses very simplistic reasoning and often faulty logic to structure and formulate what the child believes are the best set of automatic decisions for the its mind to follow from then on.

In a computer there are "macros." A macro is a set of commands for the computer to automatically set into action by a single command or combination of a few key strokes. A Core Belief is a strongly held opinion that functions much like a macro. Once it is activated (operant) it sets into action a whole chain of internal and external events, much of it sub-conscious.

So, a Core Belief is a form of automatic decision that:

May always have been valid.

May never have been valid – but seemed to be, when taken on as valid.

May only be partially valid for a particular time and circumstance.

With that in mind, consider the following concepts:

1. Individuals take on Core Beliefs at various times in their lives. These are decisions, concepts, ideas and

attitudes that become deeply integrated, and control the individual's thoughts, feelings, actions and physiology – similar to a line of code in a computer. "My sister gets a lot of love and attention from the family each time she goes to the hospital. [Sister has birth defect]. Therefore, that is the best way to get love and attention, and so I need to get sick when I want love."

2. Core Beliefs may be the same or different from one's conscious Beliefs. If they differ, the operant Core Belief will be the one in control and it will function automatically (Automatic Decision).

EX: Conscious Belief: Love is being close, tender, caring, sharing, working out differences.

Core Belief: Love is being close, caring, sharing, fighting like my parents did.

Thus this individual keeps encountering the Core Belief type of love and if s/he gets the conscious Belief about love, s/he will somehow sabotage it, lose the other person or convert the other person to performing according to the Core Belief.

3. Change the operant Core Belief and whatever thoughts, feelings, actions and physiology are controlled by that particular Core Belief will shift in line with the new Core Belief—providing no other Core Beliefs are involved in maintaining the old pattern. Sharon's Core Belief is: "to be peaceful and quiet means I am dead." She has great difficulty meditating, often can not sit still and experiences sudden unexplainable episodes of rapid heart beat. When she coverts the Core Belief that to be peaceful and quiet enhances her health and her life, she finds it much easier to meditate, sit calmly and at ease for long periods of time and her cardiac symptoms have disappeared.

4. A Core Belief is always meant to help! In accordance with the individual's experiences, logical skills, naiveté, sophistication and knowledge *at the time* of the Core Experience, the Core Belief is the best solution the individual could come up with under the circumstances *at that time!*

5. When a Core Belief is activated, the individual will think, feel, act and physiologically function at the thuse age s/he was when the Core Belief was first taken on. And feel helpless to change it! In a sense it resembles a temporary trance state. When an individual is fully into experiencing and expressing an obviously childish behavior, quietly ask them: "How old do you feel?" Often times they will stop and give an age under 8 or 9.

6. Personal Superstitions and Myths: Core Beliefs that are false, obsolete, immature, mythological or personal superstitions, will be the true source of undesirable patterns of thoughts, feelings, actions and physiological functioning as the individual goes through the ensuing years. We never mess up our lives with nice, logical, adult reasoning because logical reasoning is always distorted by the operant Core Beliefs.

   Ex: "The only way I can stay alive is to not attract attention to myself." Since the individual is now 40 years old, that seems to prove this superstition.

7. Thus the constellations of symptoms, including those that are usually given a medical or psychiatric diagnosis, are considered to be the "reflection" or result of specific Core beliefs.

8. Core Beliefs may be divided into "life enhancing" or "life limiting." Life Enhancing: "The way you show love to each other is by hugging and telling each other how much you care about them. You support each other in whatever they do to develop more of their talents and

abilities." Life Limiting: "The way you show love to each other is to scream and holler and call names and then make up. It is important that you don't do better than they do, or they better than you do. That is being selfish!"

9. An individual may believe a particular Core Belief is life enhancing and will automatically strive to follow it. If in truth the Core Belief is actually life limiting; it will still be followed automatically. The Core Beliefs are like automatic decisions that are suddenly in your mind to be taken into account when you are being logical. Gerard never seems to get to enjoy his successes. Every time he accomplishes something, he is suddenly overwhelmed with worry and guilt. The Core Belief, the automatic decision, that arises at such times is that when he feels successful he needs to feel worry and guilt. Its purpose is to prevent him from feeling happy which he believes will result in great harm to him.

10. Life limiting Core Beliefs will always be found to be the cause of any problem. The problem will always turn out to be a mal-adaptive solution, or at least some part of a mal-adaptive solution.

Example:

A. John thinks he believes that marriage is warmth, closeness, intimacy, joy, togetherness and living happily ever after.

B. John's Core Belief about marriage: "Marriage is the way my parents' marriage was—arguing, pain, separation, moments of joy and happiness and intimacy." Consequently, John hungers for what he thinks he believes marriage is (A), but his marriages are all as described in (B). If he gets into a marriage that is not like (B), and may be exactly like (A), he will somehow sabotage that relationship until it falls in line with his Core Belief (B).

29

11. All Core Beliefs have at least one memory that seems to prove the Core Belief is valid. We call such memories: "Reference Memories." It is important to realize that no memory is 100% accurate and the beliefs and interpretations attached to such memories may be nothing more than childhood myths and superstitions carried on into adulthood.

A Memory Is as Real as a Memory Is as Real as a Memory

What is the difference between the memory of an event in a dream and the memory of a childhood event "in real life" or any memory—even one about what happened a few minutes ago? Only the beliefs, the definitions, the labels attached to the memory. Otherwise there is no difference. It is commonly accepted today that anything the individual intensely imagines will be accepted by his/her mind as having actually happened. This is often encountered where one vividly rehearses what s/he is going to say to another person and then has the "memory" of already having done so. The other person is unaware of this and is surprised when the first individual acts as though the discussion has already taken place. Reference Memories are those memories we used to prove our Core Beliefs are true. The younger one is when storing such a memory, the more distorted is the memory. The more upset one is when storing such a memory, the more distorted the memory.

We tend to live our lives based on beliefs based on a distorted past. To compound the felony, we use that reference memory to predict our future and how to handle it. It is important to get a sense of this because we tend to use such reference memories as being 100% true, and direct our lives from the past – as we remember it – with our childhood interpretations, understandings and definitions connected to such references.

Consequently, our past becomes prologue to our future. We consciously and unconsciously structure our future based on the way we remember our past and the Core Beliefs connected to those memories. Our future results from self-fulfilling prophecy rather than unfolding spontaneously.

This understanding of the falseness of memory is also important in coming to forgiveness, which we will discuss in more detail in Chapter Eleven.

The Problem Profile Technique

The Problem Profile is a simple, easy, non-threatening set of questions to enable you to focus more accurately on the cause of the problem or challenge. It is easiest, and most effective, to simply take the answers that "pop" into mind rather than doing a lot of thinking about them.

1. Problem: What seems to be the problem?
2. Onset: When did this problem first start?
3. Earliest Onset: What was going on in your life about that time?
4. Effects: Please tell me all the ways in which the problem affects your life?

   A. What does it cause you to do or not do?
   B. What does it cause you to feel or not feel?
   C. What does it cause others to do or not do?
   D. What does it cause others to feel or not feel?

5. Life Different: Supposing your problem was completely gone—out of your life forever. Please list all the ways you and your life would be different.

6. Concerns: Taking the first thought that comes to mind, when you think about this problem being completely gone forever, what fears, guilts, doubts, worries or anxieties come to mind about no longer having it in your life?

7. Benefits: As you think about all this, is there any way in which having this problem has been a blessing in disguise, even though it has been causing you a lot of problems?

8. Keep: What do you do that keeps the problem continuing in your life?

9. Does there seem to be a connection between having this problem and what was going on in your life, as answered in question #3? (Can you see how having the problem may have been a "solution" to what was going on then?)

NOTE: Answers to Question #6 indicates what you are trying to avoid by having the problem.

Answers to Question #7 indicates what you are trying to keep or gain by having the problem.

Focusing on correcting these aspects often results in eliminating the chief complaint.

Summary of the Problem Profile

The Problem Profile provides a format for eliciting key points of the psycho-dynamics of the presenting complaint. After only one session with the Problem Profile, most individuals will have a sense that the presenting complaint may be an obsolete solution for another, more basic, problem. Thus, getting a clearer understanding of the problem may immediately reduce feelings of helplessness that usually accompany the presenting complaint.

Often this occurs because it points you in a more accurate direction as to what aspects of your thinking to work with.

Repeated profiles may be done on each of the Concerns and Benefits for even better understanding of your thinking.

Instinctoid Needs

Some years ago, Abraham Maslow co-founded Humanistic Psychology. He based his work on studying "above normal" individuals. He believed they exemplified what humans are capable of, rather than simply being "normal." Lincoln, Washington, and many others, resulted in his formulating the concept of the "self actualized individual."

The "self actualized individual" is the individual who automatically functions on superior levels of life. Not so much because they are smarter, but because they use more of their talents and abilities. One question he consistently asked his classes: "Some one has to be the best at what you do, why not you?"

As the authors continued to work with Core Beliefs, it became increasingly obvious that when limiting Core Beliefs were upgraded or eliminated, the individual automatically moved into higher levels of functioning. Thanks to Dr. Jean Houston,[18] we realized that this phenomenon was best described by the term: "Entelechy."

We define Entelechy as "the full expression of one's potential. The fulfillment of the innate drive to be the highest and finest one is capable of being." We think this drive exists within every conscious thing.

---

[18] Personal communication – 1975

When we seek to help others realize their entelechy we are seeking to help them become "fully actualized" or, using all of their potential.

Maslow created a hierarchy of basic and meta needs. We found, clinically, that there was a different order of importance and a more practical way of listing such needs.

Therapeutically, the idea is that if each of these basic needs is important, then the Core Belief defining each of these needs and how each of these needs is satisfied is most important.

Consequently, we can use these Instinctoid Needs, and the individual's particular Core Beliefs about each need, therapeutically.

We have listed these Instinctoid needs according to order of importance as demonstrated to us by our clients.

Instinctoid Needs in Order of Strength and Importance:

1. Autonomy
2. Physical Survival
3. Safety and Security
4. Acceptance and Belonging
5. Giving and Receiving Love including sexual expressions
6. Self Esteem – self worth, self love
7. Spiritual – a sense of a Higher Power or Universal Wisdom in one's life

Traditionally, we are taught that physical survival is the most powerful need of all. The authors strongly reject this idea. The need for Autonomy, the need to have a sense of influence and control over one's life, the need to not feel helpless or powerless is so strong that we will damage our bodies in order to maintain a sense of autonomy. Just look at any list of so-called "psycho-somatic disorders."

It is axiomatic that any adult with an organic disorder, will have had at least one emotional upset or loss within three years prior to the onset of the physical pathology. On careful questioning, such an individual may quickly see how the onset of the physical disorder's symptoms was a "last ditch stand" against the overwhelming emotional impact of the preceding events.

When you look at your answers to the Concerns and Benefits questions, you may be able to categorize each of them as to what instinctoid need is involved.

Handling Uncomfortable Feelings

Your feelings are naturally designed to flow through you.

Your feelings and your emotional state are naturally designed to be:

1. Physically experienced, and
2. Consciously acted upon.

All of your feelings are naturally designed to help. No feeling is a negative feeling or harmful feeling because each feeling is naturally designed to be experienced. You just allow it to be. You just allow the feeling/emotion to flow into whatever feelings/emotions come next. It is going to go through a series of changes until you feel empty, drained or comfortable again. Finally you will discover that it leaves you feeling better. Suppose you are feeling guilty...you simply say to your self: "I am feeling what I think is (state the feeling)...I feel this uncomfortable feeling...in my (state whatever parts of your body you are feeling it in...)...just because I am feeling this way does not mean that it is true...or false...it is just a feeling I am having...and I am just allowing myself to feel this way for now"...Perhaps after a few minutes…you discover that this uncomfortable feeling has changed…and now it feels like another uncomfortable feeling…again you say: "I am feeling what I think is (state the feeling)…I feel this uncomfortable feeling in my (state parts of body)…just because I am feeling this way does not make it true…or false…it is just an uncomfortable feeling I am having about something and I am allowing myself to feel this way for now"…Perhaps after a few minutes the feeling changes again and you say to yourself…"I am feeling what I think is (state feeling)…I feel this uncomfortable feeling in my (state body parts)…just because I feel this way doesn't mean it is true or false…it is just an uncomfortable feeling I am having about something…and I am just allowing myself to feel this way for now"…Keep doing this until you find the uncomfortable feelings have gone and the feeling you are left with is comfortable or at least neutral…

If it leads you to an early event in your life—then that will be the true source of the uncomfortable feelings you are having at the time. Write them down. Somehow they will be related to the problems going on in your life now.

Chapter Three

Narcissistic Parenting

The narcissistic person is a very self centered person. They are so insecure and so focused on themselves and their needs that they act, think and feel as though nothing else exists except for their purposes. One of the most frequent causes of this extreme self centeredness is to be raised by narcissistic parents. To the young developing child, such self centeredness appears to be a form of power and control that is of great value to emulate.

Narcissus

Narcissus was the youth in the ancient myths, who looked into a reflecting pool and fell in love with himself. Narcissus, being so enamored with himself failed to hear the endlessly whispered words of Echo who loved him. Narcissus was not only ignorant of Echo, but also of his own possibilities, and has come to symbolize people who are very self-centered.

They are described as being in "love" with themselves to the exclusion of any one else; so wrapped up in themselves and what they want, that they have very little, if any concern about others. It is as though they are wearing blinders and can only see what affects them. They seem to have no idea of the pain and harm they inflict on those around them, especially their children.

Because narcissists suffer from low self esteem, fear and guilt (which they almost always pass on to their children), they may destroy nearly all the relationships they have with a spouse, child, family and friends. Because it is so important to them that the world exists for them and gives them what they want, they are great manipulators, skilled in all the various forms. Most commonly, they use guilt: "If you love Mommy, you will..."

It is absolutely right to love yourself. It is absolutely right to take care of and satisfy your own particular needs. (The narcissist would accuse you of being selfish if you did that around them.)

It becomes pathological when such love is not extended out to others; when such care is with little or no concern as to the effect on others; when such narcissistic attitudes and actions are repeatedly harmful to others. This chapter focuses on the effects upon the developing child and the pathology as seen in adulthood.

The narcissistic individual is self absorbed in what s/he wants and fears, apparently without any concern for the effect it has on others. S/he is either unable, or refuses, to understand another's protestations, complaints and pain, if it interferes with the narcissist's desires.

The narcissistic parent is one who uses his or her children in manipulative ways to try to fulfill the parent's needs with little, if any, regard as to the effect on the child.

The narcissistic family is one which tries to control each member so they fit in with the overall dictates of the family in much the same way as the narcissistic parent.

While the following discussion will refer to the parental figure as the "narcissistic mother," the reader should stay aware that it can be any parental figure and/or the family grouping, who is perceived as having the control over the individual Too, a dominant sister or brother in a household with passive parents may have the same effect as a narcissistic parent. And, of course, an entire family or community may be that way:

"If you want to be a member of this family (if you want to survive and be taken care of by us, if you want to belong and be acceptable) you will have an honest man's job, and not be one of those gray suited hot shots."

Copying

Children growing up with a narcissist may consciously and unconsciously copy that behavior. To the child, it seems to be a way to achieve a powerful autonomy. Thus, they too, put the world and their children into double bind behavior. Or they may copy the other parent believing that if the dominant parent "loves" the other person, then they will love the child accordingly. Or they may copy the dominant parent believing that if they are like the dominant parent, then the dominant parent will love them for being that way and treat them differently than before.

And so the "sins of the first generation are visited unto the third generation."

Victims, raising victims, raising victims. Usually the children of the third generation refuse to follow certain family teachings. Sometimes because their parents have made a conscious effort not to raise their children the way they were raised.

Categories of Narcissistic Parenting

Practically speaking, there are three basic types of narcissists; however, there may be combinations and, of course, there are those of a tight knit family or community or religion.

To the young, developing child, "fitting in with the family" is a life or death decision. To no longer be a member of one's family means total abandonment. The child is well aware that it can not survive without someone to take care of it. So, "you fit in with the family" or die.

Stage Mother:

This description is well known to most people. The mom who always wanted to be a movie star and pushes her daughter into attempting to do the same thing. The dad who always wanted to be a super sport star and pushes his son into striving to do the same thing. The key factor here is whether the child really wants to do this, or is only doing so in order to please the parent. If, at a later date, the child decides it does not want to continue the grind, the parent should honor those wishes fully. The Stage Mother will not. S/he will use every means of coercion, guilt and manipulation so this parent's dream is not lost – again.

The child may grow up believing that it needs to be under pressure in order to do well or prove itself to the world.

The child is exhorted to be, do and succeed at what the Stage Mother was not able to do herself. Within limits, this is all right if the child really enjoys the promotion and it is what the child really wants to do. However, the pathological Stage Mother is constantly exhorting the child to do more and better. The relationship is superficially one of love and encouragement, but underneath is the mother's need: "You have to do increasingly better because that means I am doing increasingly better." Or, "I am important because I made you what you are."

The Queen:

This parent acts as though the only purpose the child has is to take care of that parent, and be an extension of that parent, to serve that parent and to have no life, goals or desires other than tending to that parent's wants and needs: "I could only do, be and have what my mother decreed." A child growing up with such a parent fully understands what Cinderella was experiencing with her family.

If the child takes on Survival Dependency, it fears not being an extension of that parent. To take care of that there will always be some reason to be frequently involved with the narcissistic parent: "Mom's getting on in years and somebody has to check her each day and do for her." Such ongoing involvement may be directly with that parent or by marrying an individual who has certain characteristics in common with that parent.

John was a young musician whose father died early in his life, leaving John with a narcissistic mother to grow up with. Because his father died when John was 6 years old, John was quite concerned about not losing his mother. He was angry at his father and God because his father "left" him alone. So began a long term, low level depression. His mother was constantly admonishing him. How he was to act, say, think, feel. All of these messages were focused around what he was to do for her.

By the time he was a teenager he began to rebel, and dressed and acted quite differently from her. At the annual family reunions his long hair and hippie clothes opened him up to criticism from the adults there, as they thought he should look and be as they did.

As an adult, his mother, her royal highness, the queen, would say to him, "You don't need to drive to that doctor you've been seeing. Besides, your car is having problems and you can't drive it too far. I want you to stay home and take me to your Aunt Jane's. Then I'll call you when I am ready to come home." Much later on, he realized that he had become a survival dependent – with her as the Protector/Rescuer/Caretaker. This too, had to be redefined.

Eventually in therapy, John learned that he wasn't a trapped child, and he didn't need to feel guilty when he wouldn't let his mother control his life for her benefit. As he began to assert himself with her, setting limits and boundaries as to what he would do or would not do for her or with her, she became even more demanding. She tried even harder to keep him in the old pattern.

John had been warned about this and was prepared. He had learned that he could say, "No, I won't do that," <u>and not have to defend his refusal</u>. When he defended his refusal, his reasons for refusing were attacked, and then those responses were attacked.

The usual outcome was to wear John down so he would give in.

However, once John set the limits and boundaries as to what he would do and how he would allow others to treat him, this could no longer occur. He would say "no" and not defend his refusal. Eventually the others, including his mother, learned that he could no longer be manipulated, so they accepted his decisions.

Attacker:

This type of narcissistic parent is unable to tolerate any evidence that his or her child may be smarter, cleverer, more lovable, better looking, etc. than the parent. This often shows up in indirect ways, such as cheating in order to win a game the parent is playing with the child. Such a parent may find a variety of ways to not recognize any of the child's accomplishments. In other forms of attack, such a parent will never give the child any complements about anything the child does and often insults or attacks the child and/or the child's accomplishments.

Unfortunately the child usually sees this as something wrong with himself rather than the parent. This may result in the child striving all the harder and doing better. Of course this, in turn, brings more attacks upon the child. In very direct attacks, such a parent will consistently blame, criticize, lie about, and even physically abuse the child in order to keep the child from looking, doing or being better than this parent. The child quickly learns a painful lesson: it is dangerous to make the parent wrong in any way.

Parents playing the role of "Devil's Advocate" are experienced by the child as attackers of his/her ability to make good decisions.

Direct Attacker

The direct attacker is very obvious, and eventually the child goes to great lengths to not attract the direct attacker's attentions.

The direct attacker will ridicule the child's accomplishments.

The direct attacker may actually sabotage the child's school projects by "helping the child out." However such help results in the child's project doing poorly at school.

D. B.'s father, a scientific genius, was highly infantile, manipulative and competitive for the mother's attention. He could not tolerate D.B. being praised or doing well in the mother's eyes. Offering to help with her science fair project, he did some things that resulted in a great deal of problems at the fair. She had the project all worked out and ready to go. He decided he was going to show her how to do it. He suggested some things that were not allowed by the fair. She told him so and he told her it wouldn't make any difference, she would win. The outcome, of course, was that she was blamed for his dishonesty and the project was rejected from the competition. If D. B. had been allowed to do it her way, there would have been no problems.

Indirect Attacker:

This type of narcissist is much more subtle and just as damaging to the developing child. Eventually the child learns that it is not to do anything which gives the indirect attacker grounds to subtly attack. "Look Dad, we had to spell one hundred words and I spelled every one correctly. Look at what my teacher wrote on my paper." Dad: "Humph, what's the big deal, you are supposed to get them

43

all right. That's what I send you to school for." Often the same individual will attack both directly and indirectly.

Combinations of two or more of these three types. There is also the parent who is so aloof from its children that the children wonder what they did that s/he has no interaction with them. This parent may be physically present in the home, but does not communicate except to say, "Pass the salt," and has no direct physical contact with the child. Naturally this parent's children blame themselves.

Consider the mother who expresses her narcissism in the form of concern for the child. "Son, your car is too old to make those 35-mile trips to your doctor, so just stay home, drive me to your Aunt Ethel's and wait until I phone you to pick me up. She lives only 5 miles away." (This was actually reported by a young man.) Or the parent who is very kind and loving while the child is doing exactly what is wanted, such as in a "stage mother" situation, and then becomes an indirect attacker with snide remarks, insults and comments when the child expresses interest in some other area.

Brian Wilson's[19] father, Murray, is described as an intensely narcissistic parent who once said to Brian that he (Brian) was a winner, so go out there and win! Some months later Brian was due to get a BMI award and his father accused him of getting a fat head.[20] The stage mother aspect was the great lengths Murray went to encourage his son's success in his music. The attacker aspect came out because of Murray's jealousy over his son's accomplishments.

---

[19] of the famed Beach Boys

[20] *The Nearest Faraway Place*, Timothy White, Henry Holt & Co., NY, NY, 1994 (This biography is an excellent documentation of victims, raising victims, raising victims, and the devastation of the family.)

Family/Environmental:

Consider the position taken in this way:

"If you want to be a member of this family, you must earn your money with your hands and not dress in those fancy clothes!"

In such circumstances, the message is: "If you want to be a member of this family you will fit in with our choices for you."

Or, the narcissistic parent taking a position against certain types of friendships or loving alliances because they are seen as a threat. "Yes, I know you think you love that girl, but she is not good enough for you! She doesn't fit in to our kind of life. Just be patient and I'll let you know when the right one shows up."

Thus, the child, now an adult, is not allowed to form outside attachments.

If a marriage does occur involving a "mama's boy," it is described at the time of the divorce as a threesome: "I married him and his mother."

Tacit Promise or Threat

Practically speaking, the type of narcissistic parent is academic. The key factor is the young, developing child's perception and responses to such an environment. This results in the child coming to certain decisions that are designed to insure survival and become automatic: taking on certain limiting Core Beliefs that function as Automatic Decisions. Each of the Core Beliefs involved will contribute to the child's concept as to what is required for the child to survive in the environment s/he is growing up in.

The child, at first, usually does all it can to please the parent and to get the parent's love and attention. Such activity eventually passes out of enjoyment and into pain, criticism, fear and mixed feelings of love and hate. The child does not want to disappoint the narcissistic parent; does not want to cause the narcissistic parent to become angry at the child. In the child's mind, the narcissistic parent has made a promise to the child – whether or not the parental figure is aware of it.

Reward For Being Unreal

There seems to be a promise, tacit or clear, that <u>if</u> the child sets aside its own feelings and desires; if the child becomes as the parent orders, something of benefit will occur for the child. Such a promise may be desirable, such as expressions of love; or as a threat, such as withdrawing from the child.

Whether promise or threat, the child learns to become "unreal." Because to feel, do, be and have other than what the narcissist orders may literally be a death threat to the young, developing child. The narcissist is usually totally unaware that the child has come to believe such an agreement between the two of them exists.

The narcissist may never have indicated in any way, any promise of something better for the child. Yet it is not uncommon for the child to work it out in his/her mind that something of great benefit will occur. This is a "carrot," a reward, a pay-off as the child whittles down the expression of who and what s/he is. Fortunately, however, like a glowing ember of coal hidden deep within the ashes of a fire, the real person waits to be freed.

The stage mother may have wanted to be a movie star or great musician or tennis player and never made it. She pushes the child from early on to be, do and have what the mother couldn't. Then the mother feels like she has finally succeeded. If the child doesn't succeed in getting the part, or never really becomes a star, the narcissistic stage mother may psychologically whip the child for such seeming failure by withholding the "promise" or enacting the "threat," regardless of the cost to the child. The "Stage Mother" is often quite aware of the promised rewards she has offered the child. S/he is also quite aware of the threats that have been promised.

Another common message is that whatever the child is doing is never good enough. The child may put forth great thought and effort into trying to please this parent (so the parent won't kill the child or abandon it), but never receives that anticipated reward. The child soon wants to escape from all the pressure the narcissistic parent is putting on the child. Eventually, suicide may be the final solution. Like many solutions developed by the young, developing child a strange dichotomy occurs. In this case, the child is striving to be everything the narcissist demands so it won't be abandoned and die. It then takes on that the only escape is to die. In other words, killing itself so it won't die.

Every clinician is aware of at least one highly talented child who is dead before graduating high school: a child whose family had such high hopes, and either expressed or implied demands, that this child is to go out and be and do wonderful things. And then, the child dies in an auto accident, or from a sudden fatal disease, etc. The child experiencing such high expectations just has too much to live up to.

Everyone has heard of the child with the narcissistic parent who wants her to become a doctor, then during her first year of medical school she commits suicide. This happens because it is the only way out from under the narcissistic parent's pressure for the child to achieve. If the narcissistic parent is a Stage Mother, then she is trying to vicariously get, via the child, what the parent could not do for himself or herself. The narcissistic parent trying to live his or her life through the child and the child's achievements and so, considering the child's achievement as his or her own.

Such a parent ignores the child's true desires, wants and needs to feel, do, be or have something else. It is as though the child has become an extension of the Stage Mother narcissist, for such a parent has great difficulty in seeing herself and the child as being two separate individuals. Any emotions the child has that does not fit in with the narcissist's desires is immediately directly, or indirectly, attacked: "Oh, you just think you are unhappy because you couldn't go with them."

The Queen narcissistic parent, is a world class expert at using love and guilt as tools to manipulate the child into taking care of the parent's wants and needs. The child comes to believe that if they love the parent (or anyone else) then the child must wait on them, do their bidding; Thus, becoming their servant in one form or another. Often the child carries this into adulthood and finds himself or herself in relationships where they are waiting hand and foot on the loved one. Often they unconsciously select self-centered people to be attracted to and fall in love with. Or they will pick people, to be attracted to and fall in love with, who need to be rescued or taken care of, because this fits in with the child's, (now an adult) definition of love. In other words, the spouse becomes the narcissistic parent, symbolically.

Unfinished Business

In such an instant, the child has "unfinished business" with this parent in the need to get acknowledgement, acceptance, love and or accomplishment. "If I could have just got him to say he loved me, or that he was proud of me."

Consequently, this unfinished business will drive the individual to be involved in love relationships where the other party somehow represents the parent.

The individual unconsciously believes that if they can't get love/acceptance/acknowledgement from the one parent, s/he can symbolically get it from some other parental figure – a symbolic parental figure.

Since the other figure behaves like the parental figure in a key manner, the attempt is doomed to failure.

The reader should be aware that there are other circumstances in which unfinished business, and the relationship disasters it creates, may occur besides within the Triad.

Keep in mind that the Adult Child of a Narcissistic Parent is struggling to avoid thinking, feeling and doing according to who and what s/he really is, but at the same time wants to find out "my true identity," and function accordingly. A self-inflicted double bind.

Until the operant Core Beliefs are accessed and eliminated or upgraded, s/he will more or less function as his/her "unreal self."

Unfortunately, as the various uncomfortable feelings arise, the Adult Child of Narcissistic Parents looks to his/her present situation to explain such feelings. While s/he may develop explanations for such feelings based on present events, the truth is that such feelings are "partial memories" arising without the mental images that show their true source.

A Word About Partial Memory

A Partial Memory is the actively recalled memory of an event but, unlike the usual memory, only the various feelings are experienced, no pictures! The individual experiences only the feelings. Because s/he does not access the "pictures" that identify the memory, s/he may try to explain such feelings as the result of something happening in the present.

Ex: You are sitting in your yard enjoying the sunshine and the flowers. Suddenly you feel a mild anxiety and a sense of guilt accompanying that anxiety. If you are like many people, you start wondering what you did that day that is causing you to feel guilty. You then start remembering the various events of the day and finally settle on: having being rude to the grocery clerk.

That explains it. It probably doesn't relieve the uncomfortable feelings much, but eventually they fade away. If the rudeness was the cause, recalling the rudeness and dealing with it ordinarily will cause the anxiety and the guilt to quickly disappear. If you have a Core Belief that you are being selfish if you just sit around relaxed and enjoying the view when you really should be busy with something else, the anxiety and guilt are a partial memory recall of when you where made to feel that way as a child simply enjoying yourself. The real cause of the anxiety and guilt was the triggering of a Core Belief which says: "You should feel anxious and guilty if you are sitting around doing nothing. Remember what your father told you about that?"

An individual may have a memory triggered that consists of mother criticizing him and the fear he felt. If it comes up as a Partial Memory, he will feel the fear but not see any of the pictures showing the event that is being partially recalled. Suddenly feeling a sense of guilt, but unconsciously repressing the childhood memory of mother criticizing him. Thus he then examines what is going on in present time and blame those guilt feelings on some aspect of the present, rather than realizing they are a censored memory. The emotions are allowed up from the past but the event itself is censored out.

The child growing up with a narcissist is often emotionally abused and deprived. Deprived of the physical and verbal expressions that s/he is loved, cared about and respected for who and what s/he really is; deprived of a sense of accomplishment and individuality.

Symptoms

1. Chronic sadness varying in intensity from occasional spontaneous feelings of sadness to full blown depression. This may be interrupted with outbursts of energy, effort and emotional surges In the extreme, as seen in Manic-Depressive conditions.

2. Chronic recurrent feelings of guilt, also varying in intensity and spontaneity. Often as children they felt guilty even though they were not the guilty person. Some of these children will admit guilt, even though they were innocent, explaining they were protecting a sibling: "I could handle the punishment better than my sister could." Or that "negative" attention is better than no attention: "At least that way they had to recognize that I was around."

3. A sense that they can never do anything good enough. That no matter how hard they try to be "perfect" (whatever that means), they fail. A variation of this is feeling "undeserving," especially if they get something they really want.

4. A Belief that they are unlovable and can never be loved for who and what they really are: "I know I am not loveable otherwise my parents would never have treated me the way they did. I am still trying to figure out what there is about me that no one can love me."

5. Acceptance of deprecating labels thrown at them during times of great emotional interaction, and acting them out according to their beliefs as to what each of these labels means. For example, being called "bad," "stupid," "ugly," or a "failure" may result in the individual functioning as though such labels were true,

51

for fear of making the parent wrong: "My father said I was nothing but a whore so I decided I might as well be one."

6. A sense of helplessness; having no control over one's life.

7. In the more extreme cases, the Adult Child Of Narcissistic Parents feels that s/he will be killed or otherwise disposed of, if s/he feels or acts more themselves. Some instances of multiple personality may have their roots here as this becomes a powerful defense in the mind of the child. After all, if Jill becomes "Jane" then she is not breaking parental law, "Jane" is the culprit.

8. Chronic anger and rage ranging from full repression to spontaneous violent outbursts. The child of the narcissistic parent becomes very adept at controlling the anger towards the parent, because as a child s/he came to believe that if it is released s/he will kill the parent. Depression is the anesthetic used for this. It is not uncommon to encounter manic-depressives who were raised in highly narcissistic circumstances. The authors' limited experience with such individuals indicates that this may be the pre-dominant cause of that kind of depression. Human beings were not designed to be like the Vulcan, Mr. Spock, who functioned as a very logical, unemotional creature.[21] Repression of feelings of helplessness and anger sooner or later result in physical symptoms and organic pathology.

9. Chronic low-grade depression or worse. The various factors involved are guaranteed to cause the child to go through life with an underlying sense of sadness or

---

[21] Interestingly, according to Star Trek episodes, even Vulcans go through a periodic experience of overwhelming emotions. During a mating season they are unable to think clearly and will fight anyone to the death that gets in the way of the mating ritual.

much worse. Consequently, the Adult Child Of Narcissistic Parents goes through life with at least a vague, underlying feeling of sadness. Such individuals may comment on being aware of the sadness, yet not able to understand why.

10. Poor relationships. This includes love relationships, business relationships, committee work, etc. They never learned how to have a true sharing relationship during childhood, where would they learn it in adulthood?

11. Inability to set limits and boundaries as to how, and to what extent, they will let others treat them. Such as: letting others treat them in inconsiderate ways, make unfair demands on them, trying to be perfect to fit in with someone else's definition of them, etc. If the narcissistic parent discovers the adult child is in therapy, that parent usually engages in a very powerful attempt to separate the adult child from the therapy.

12. A constant need to be reassured in some way that s/he is loved and cared about. Many individuals become Survival Dependent[22] as a way of constantly having someone else fill the role of the narcissistic parent and Thus result in a "safe" environment. The Adult Child of Narcissistic Parents seems to avoid doing, being or having anything that has not been decided or encouraged by some one else. This way the Adult Child Of Narcissistic Parents believes it can avoid blame and attack for the outcome of any decision.

13. Unconsciously reacting to authority figures (teachers, employers, ministers, etc.) as being the narcissistic parent symbolically. This is usually the result of a Belief that such automatic categorizing will make things easier for the child, now an adult, to function in that

---

[22] Spear, "Survival Dependency," *Journal of the American Academy of Medical Hypnoanalysts*, June,1996 Vol. XI, No. 2 (See also Chapter Eight on Survival Dependency.)

setting. However, it results in the Adult Child Of Narcissistic Parent spontaneously regressing to child-like thinking and behavior when interacting with that individual. Such spontaneous regression is an automatic, trance-like state as the individual functions under the activated Core Beliefs that it believes enabled it to survive with the narcissistic parent. This is an automatic decision process.

14. Fear of one's real emotions. The child quickly learns that it is only allowed to feel and express those emotions decreed by the narcissistic parent. Any other emotions are either deprecated or attacked: "Oh, Johnny, you only think you are unhappy. Mother knows what's best for you." Failure to hide one's real emotions almost always results in some kind of attack: "We were sitting at the dinner table, my older brothers and my parents. I was feeling sad because of a dead cat I saw in the road earlier that day. Mom asked me what was wrong and I started to cry as I told her about the cat. My brothers and my Father began to call me 'crybaby,' and other names, until I ran from the table. Although I had realized it before, from then on I knew I really had to hide whatever I was feeling."

15. Development of a facade. Initially the child consciously develops a facade to present to the narcissistic parent. Over a period of time, the child, now an adult, may come to believe that s/he is, in reality, this facade. The "real self" is being buried or compartmentalized in a private dungeon in the non-conscious mind. (Fortunately it is never completely dead!)

16. Conflicting love/hate emotions towards the narcissistic parent and anyone symbolizing that parent.

17. Difficulty making decisions. This is usually the avoidance of making a decision for fear that it will be wrong and the narcissistic parent will withhold the promise and/or bring on the attack.

18. A need to be perfect. That is, "perfect" as defined by the narcissistic parent: "I soon realized that my mother wanted me to be a perfect little girl. This meant I had to be 'good.' 'Good' girls don't make any loud noises, don't ask questions, don't cause any problems; 'good' meant *don't.*"

19. A sense of being "invisible." This often comes about by the parent discussing the child as though the child was not in the same room, and/or the child yearning to be invisible in order to escape the attention of the narcissistic parent.

20. Chronic substance abuse ranging from food to smoking tobacco to various drugs, legal and illegal. Such abuse may be acts of autonomy: "They can dictate everything else I do, but they can't stop me from doing this." Or it may be a temporary means of coping with the enormous internal pressures of the conflict. The reader might keep in mind that any substance abuse from heroin to cigarettes to alcohol to food is to serve one or both of two purposes – to get a feeling and/or to avoid a feeling. This is also a short term means of getting some pleasure in an acceptable way, because it is followed by pain and suffering, including guilt. Thus the side effects after the pleasure wears off is a penitence and a means of staying in the "tension."

21. The unconscious use of physical illness with true organic pathology as a means of controlling any movement out of the "unreal self." This may result from following a Core Belief that says, "The only time I get any love or attention is when I am sick. So if I am sick, not only will I stay the way she wants me to be, I will also get some kind of love and attention from her and others." It may also be a physically limiting solution so the Adult Child of Narcissistic Parents is physically prevented from certain activity. Then the narcissist cannot expect the usual obedience from the child.

Darlene came to the office for depression, but had a crippling arthritis which prevented her from writing and flying up to San Francisco where her demanding mother lived. It was soon discovered that the arthritis was specifically developed to avoid having to write the mother daily and to avoid flying to San Francisco to see her. When she learned she was no longer a child and could say "no" the arthritis was greatly relieved. At the time she stopped therapy she still had about 5% of the arthritis left. When she was asked about that, she said it was "just in case." It was a kind of insurance as a "last ditch stand" against her mother –if she ever needed it.

William, a 20 yr old was covered with lesions and scabs of psoriasis. It was discovered that the purpose of the skin condition was to prevent others from physically touching him. Learning to handle that in other ways resulted in almost total disappearance of the disease.

Shirley had extremely serious pre-menstrual tension. It often put her in bed for several days and not going out of her apartment for almost a week. It was revealed that this was the only way she believed she could get people to leave her alone. When she learned other ways of doing that, the pre-menstrual tension completely disappeared.

Rearing one's children more or less using the same narcissistic attitudes and practices as the parent. In effect, the Adult Child Of Narcissistic Parents becomes a narcissistic parent himself/herself and often is totally unaware of it. Again, victims, raising victims, raising victims.

22. Acting as the narcissistic parent in supervising employees and co-workers. In a sense this is subjecting the world to the same narcissistic demands the Adult Child Of Narcissistic Parents was raised in, because it seem to the young, developing child that was the way to exercise control, power and autonomy.

23. Children growing up in a strongly narcissistic environment may have difficulty developing a sense of identity separate from the narcissistic parent. Often they may have feelings of not being real, seen or heard unless the child is doing exactly what the narcissistic parent wants, in the exact way the narcissistic parent wants it. The child may be in the same room with the narcissistic parent, listening to the narcissistic parent talk about the child as though the narcissistic parent is talking about himself or herself, or as though the child wasn't there. The Adult Child Of Narcissistic Parents may have a strong feeling of not knowing how to think, feel and be in the world without the narcissistic parent available. Thus, staying connected, in a needy way, to the very person they fear the most. See "Zelda" in Chapter Eight.

24. The child may feel consumed by the narcissistic parent, perhaps even feeling invisible or unreal due to such treatment. And so, the child feels even more encouraged to not be his or her real self but, perhaps instead, to mimic, to copy someone else. And, who that model is to be, is strongly influenced by the narcissistic parent.

25. Narcissistic parenting leaves the child with feelings of loneliness, emptiness, self doubt, inadequacy, of never being good enough, difficulty in fitting in, being something one is not, in order to please the narcissistic parent. Perhaps feelings of being out of place, chronically angry, incapable, lost, helpless, trapped, a sense of being unreal, of being a copy or an instrument of the narcissistic parent. Also, feelings of great guilt that they are never quite right, that the child is never good enough, that the child is undeserving, that the child is causing the narcissistic parent pain by not meeting the criteria the narcissistic parent desires and commands; that the child has desires different from than those of the narcissistic parent, and fear. The child has

not really learned what is right or wrong, good or bad, etc. in the sense of true values, but only what seems to help the child lessen the narcissistic parent's displeasure. Survival is paramount, yet the attempts at survival may strongly contribute to the guilt.

26. Living in fear. Fear of the narcissistic parent's displeasure, of not being able to survive if the child shifts out of the desires of the narcissistic parent, and tries to do, be and have what the child wants to do, be and have. Fear that s/he is not doing what is expected in the way the narcissistic parent orders, cajoles, or may otherwise indicate to the child. And fear that the child may lose control of itself and lash out devastatingly attacking the parent. More about this in Chapter Seven: Lizzie Borden Rage.

Narcissistic parents often put the child in double binds.[23] Telling the child that s/he can do, be and have what ever s/he wants and then insisting that the child do, be and have exactly what the narcissistic parent wants. Or, a child living part of the year with one parent who insists it be one way, and then living the rest of the year with the other parent who insists that it be quite the opposite way.

Narcissistic parents cannot love the child for who and what the child really is. The Stage Mother can only love the child as a reflection of themselves. They can only love the child when the child is being as they themselves wanted to be. The Queen requires servants, and the Attacker is terrified of the child's abilities. The narcissist will take every step s/he can think of to control those in their world accordingly.

---

[23] "The Double Bind," Spear, J & C., *Medical Hypnoanalysis Journal*, Vol. XI, No. 4, December, 1996 (See also the Chapter Four on Double Binds.)

Often a second double bind occurs in that the child is trapped between wanting to be what s/he really is and the knowledge that s/he is never going to be allowed to discover what that is. This Core Belief often interferes with achieving resolution of the problem. Commonly we hear, "What's the use."

For some children the situation is much worse, as in the case of the Attacker: the narcissistic parent who is fearful of recognizing the child as being smarter or better or prettier than the parent; fearful of acknowledging the child has done something good; jealous of any sign or evidence that the child is talented or capable in any way. To be seen as surpassing the narcissistic parent is again insuring attack and risking death, in the child's perception.

At first such children strive even harder, doing even better, and are often being far more successful in school or whatever pursuit, than the parent ever dreamed of being at that age, as a result of the narcissistic parent's treatment. Unfortunately this only causes the narcissistic parent to be even more narcissistic and increase its attacks on the child.

As the narcissist pushes for the child to succeed where s/he didn't; or attacking the child for seeming to be better than the parent, or for doing too well or making the child into some sort of servant, the child comes to believe that the only way s/he can survive is to limit himself or herself. It does this by hiding such abilities and talents that the parent discouraged. It does this by withdrawing and becoming "invisible" in hopes that now maybe the narcissistic parent will leave the child alone. Then, for the moment, the child is relatively free.

The child may withdraw, become erratic, moody, even suicidal, or on the contrary, attempt to become overly responsible; taking on responsibility for just about everything. Such feelings carrying over into adulthood long after the narcissistic parent's death because the child, now an adult, has come to believe that there is safety in being unreal. Safety in not being what, and who, s/he really is. Safety means Survival. Obviously the narcissistic parent has his or her own problems and the tiny, young developing child is unable to defend itself from them. Even later in childhood is a defense rarely possible. Consider the parent who did not let her child outdoors alone until he was 7 years old!

The important factor in these questions is that the parent or the family was demanding, unreasonable and highly limiting of the individual in these areas. These questions will immediately trigger many Adult Children of Narcissistic Parents into recalling, in great detail, the narcissistic demands placed on them in the first 10 or 15 years of life, and even now in adulthood.

Entelechial Approach

Ordinarily, the effective parent does raise the child in a manner to fit in with the parent's beliefs as to how the child should think, feel and act. However, such direction is motivated by a desire to raise the child to realize the highest and finest it is capable of. It is not uncommon for such a parent to place their own wants and needs second to the child's. The narcissistic parent's motivation is the reverse.

The Adult Child Of Narcissistic Parents has to come to the realization that escape is not only possible but imperative. S/he does not have to stay in that double bind and can let go of the past and become who and what s/he really is. It is possible, safe and imperative to set boundaries as to what one will allow others to expect of them; set boundaries as to what kind of treatment they will put up with; realize it is possible, safe, permissible and imperative to set their own goals and achieve them. It is pointed out to the individual that, "If you have survived this long being what you are not, you will do even better in life, with your life, by being who and what you really are."

For the truth is, the Adult Child Of Narcissistic Parents, on some level, knows exactly what his or her capabilities and talents are – because they have had to unconsciously access and then avoid using them over the years.

It is usually of great concern, often triggering vague to powerful feelings of fear for the adult child of a narcissist, to consider making such a drastic change after all this time. The child, now an adult, has been functioning under the narcissistic parent's promise or threat for so long, it can't even conceive that such a change is possible. So we suggest that s/he have:

"Dreams, very powerful, informative dreams…dreams in which you safely, harmlessly and successfully get in touch with…who and what you really are…discovering, uncovering, revealing to yourself…in your dreams…who and what you really are…your talents, your abilities, the areas in which you really do excel and feel good and right about…and then bring such thoughts, feelings, actions, reactions up into your outer physical world…safely…effectively…comfortably so that soon…very, very soon…at a rate you are comfortable with…in a way you are comfortable with…you will find yourself…being your self…doing what you want to do and be…with the people you want to do and be with…comfortably…successfully…happily…safely…effectively being your real self…following your own goals…and desires…which might even be similar to those the narcissistic parent had for you…only now they are your goals to satisfy and fulfill according to your needs and desires…back into the world again…no longer a zombie at the beck and call of the narcissistic parent…but easily…successfully…safely…happily…being yourself…so that soon…very, very soon…at a rate you are comfortable with…in a way you are comfortable with…you will have discovered that you really are a good…deserving…capable, talented person…"

Signs of Recovery:

As the Adult Child Of Narcissistic Parents automatically and effortlessly makes the following changes, such changes are strong evidence that s/he is being freed of such powerful childhood influences:

1. Able to set realistic boundaries and limitations on one's own actions and the actions of others.
2. The loss of spontaneous feelings of fear and guilt.
3. The loss of chronic feelings of sadness and depression.
4. Becoming more optimistic.
5. Recognizing his/her own desires and needs.
6. Setting goals and accomplishing such and following through with new goals.
7. Not easily susceptible to the wishes and demands of others to the his or her detriment and able to evaluate them calmly and accurately.

Summary:

Many emotional problems such as addiction, depression, self defeating behavior, dependent personality, etc. are treated as separate entities. If what has been described has happened to you in some way, you are well advised to seek much deeper than these superficial labels. Even though they are common diagnoses, they usually fail to reveal the true cause of the individual's problems.

Once it is confirmed that an individual is the adult child of a narcissistic parent, the focus of assistance becomes much more specific and accurate. In the authors' experience, simple "face-to- face" discussion is insufficient to effect a comfortable, rapid, effective release. Consequently, the authors always utilize mental imagery, with specific suggestions in a special mental state. In this state, the logical mind has been asked to act as an observer ONLY while the "rest of your mind, the symbol creator, the answerer of questions and the problem solver" does the corrective work.

"If I am not for myself, who will be? If I am only for myself, what am I? If not now, when?" Hillel

Handling Uncomfortable Feelings

Your feelings are naturally designed to flow through you.

Your feelings and your emotional state are naturally designed to be:

1. Physically experienced, and
2. Consciously acted upon

All your feelings are naturally designed to help. No feeling is a negative feeling or harmful feeling because each feeling is naturally designed to be experienced. You just allow it to be. You just allow the feeling/emotion to flow into whatever feelings/emotions that emotion or feeling is going to change into until you feel empty, drained or comfortable again.

Finally you will discover that it leaves you feeling better. Suppose you are feeling guilty...you simply say to your self:

"I am feeling what I think is (state the feeling)...I feel this uncomfortable feeling...in my (state whatever parts of your body you are feeling it in...)...just because I am feeling this way does not mean that it is true...or false...it is just a feeling I am having...and I am just allowing myself to feel this way for now"...Perhaps after a few minutes...you discover that this uncomfortable feeling has changed...and now it feels like another uncomfortable feeling...again you say: "I am feeling what I think is (state the feeling)...I feel this uncomfortable feeling in my (state parts of body)...just because I am feeling this way does not make it true...or false...it is just an uncomfortable feeling I am having about something and I am allowing myself to feel this way for now"...Perhaps after a few minutes the feeling changes again and you say to yourself..."I am feeling what I think is (state feeling)...I feel this uncomfortable feeling in my (state body parts)...just because I feel this way doesn't mean it is true or false...it is just an uncomfortable feeling I am having about something...and I am just allowing myself to feel this way for now"...Keep doing this until you find the uncomfortable feelings have gone and the feeling you are left with is comfortable or at least neutral. If the experience leads you to an early event in your life...then that will be the true source of the uncomfortable feelings you are having at the time. Write them down. Somehow they will be related to the problems going on in your life now.

Chapter Four

Growing Up In Double Binds

The Double Bind[24] has technically been defined as:

"…an interaction pattern characterized by 'severe limitations' imposed by paradoxical communication in an 'intensely important relationship' which results in an 'untenable situation,' but one from which its participants are 'unable to extricate themselves'…"

"It requires:

A. An intensely important relationship (parent-child being proto-typic) in which there occurs:
B. a communication involving a contradiction in levels of meaning which:
C. requires a response which, in order to be adequate, includes responding to the basic contradiction. Such a response is difficult to achieve because of the
D. denial or concealment of the contradiction which is contained in the message itself…and:
E. there is a prohibition against 'leaving the field'."

The above is a rather complicated way of saying the child is growing up "between a rock and a hard place" or "damned if it does and damned if it doesn't" and seems to have no way of escaping it.

So a "Double Bind" has three requirements:

---

[24] *Double Bind, The Foundation of the Communicational Approach to the Family*; Sluzki and Ransom, 1976, Grune and Stratton, NY, NY, pg. 114.

1. A course of action or thinking that the child is required to follow.
2. A course of action or thinking that the child is also required to follow that conflicts with #1.
3. <u>No escape: both #1 and #2 must be obeyed</u>. Being a child and dependent for survival on the parental figures, there is no escape.

It is those double binds, arising in childhood, that are the most damaging and are often automatically carried into adulthood. This is because the defenses set up have been converted into Core Beliefs. Core Beliefs that are designed by the child to maintain the child's survival. In so doing, the child has used the best reasoning it is capable of. Unfortunately, it is not the quality of reasoning it would later be able to use in adulthood. It is naïve, simplistic, distorted and limited. It often involves the child making itself and its feelings the cause of the child's problems.

The child is given two sets of commands, usually by parents or parental figures, and is expected to follow both. No discussion is allowed. Any complaints are brushed aside by the parental figure as being of no importance or result in a barrage of verbal, and sometimes physical, attacks against the child. While the two opposing commands are frequently verbalized, it is not uncommon to encounter one command being given verbally and the opposite command given non-verbally. For example, the child may be pushed away by a parent on a regular basis and yet when the child starts avoiding that parent, the parent becomes upset that the child is not coming to the parent for love.

Example: Johnny has just learned to walk. He toddles up to his mother while she is working in the kitchen and puts his arms around her leg to hug her. His mother becomes irritated at this and pushes him away. If he does this several times she may actually reach down and slap him for it or yell at him—terrifying him. Later on when she is watching television or talking with some friends, she wants to know how come he doesn't come up and give her a hug. Johnny has no way of discussing this with her. If this only happens once, there usually is no problem, but if it occurs several times, Johnny has no solution to his dilemma. He is not supposed to hug her, he is supposed to hug her. He is too young and naive to reason out when and when not to. With some parents there is no pattern as to when and when not to hug her, especially when the parent is highly erratic.

Example: John is raised on a working ranch. He is constantly told that he must learn to take care of himself and be independent and self sufficient. Other children and adults who act that way are pointed out to him as examples to be followed and used as models. At the age of three, John takes a fishing pole and goes down to the river—as he has done many times before with his older brothers. He spends a long time down there fishing, unaware that the rest of the ranch is trying to find him for fear that he has come to great harm. John goes home later that day feeling a sense of great accomplishment. He no longer needs his older brothers to take him fishing. He is showing that he can be independent and self sufficient. When he gets home, he is severely scolded and punished for going to the river alone. Because John can't understand the intricacies of what seems to be a double message: do but don't do; a double bind is established in his mind from then on.

Example: Suzy has parents who are raising her to be perfect. Everyone in the family is to be concerned about what the neighbors think of their actions. Every child in the family is supposed to be "good" which means not upsetting the parents. Every child in the family is supposed to make the same kind of decisions as the parents make. Such narcissistic parents may even teach Suzy and her siblings that any decisions they make that the parents do not agree with are "wrong." Only the decisions that the parents agree with are "right." As a consequence, Suzy may make excellent decisions, yet grows up believing that she cannot make good decisions. When she made what she thought were good decisions and they disagreed with the parents' wishes, she was told how wrong she was. Suzy may actually take on that her decisions are so bad, that she can not survive if there isn't someone else to make decisions for her, and Thus exhibits all the symptoms of Survival Dependency.

It is possible for the double bind to be inflicted by both parents almost accidentally:

Example: Carrie's mother was always encouraging her to be expressive, curious and to let herself be all she could be. Her father was always criticizing her for being "too cheeky" and wanted her to be more controlled "so other people would like her better." Since she spent prolonged periods of time with each parent separately (they were divorced), she was subjected to this rather unique double bind. About the time she had adjusted to being the way the one parent wanted, she then had to live with the other parent and adjust to their conflicting messages.

Example: Perhaps the ultimate double bind was demonstrated by W. C. Fields playing the role of a father. The father, mother and son are eating in the dining room. The son complains: "You don't love me, Dad!" The father back hands the kid across the face yelling; "I'll teach you not to say I don't love you!!"

"Homemade" Double Binds

"When you were growing up, was there a feeling or sense that you were between a rock and a hard place?"

"Was there something you were supposed to think, do, or feel and that you were also not supposed to think, do, or feel that way?"

These questions are to get a sense of whether or not the commands you were given during the developing years made you feel like you were "damned if you do and damned if you don't."

Clues to a home life containing double binds are:

1. It was not permissible to communicate your actual feelings or to even allow the parental figure to know you had certain feelings.
2. One, or both, parents or parental figures were experienced as erratic. That is, you never really knew how they were going to be when you came home from school. Or that one of them was predictable until s/he got drunk but you never knew when such would occur.
3. One or both parents had narcissistic traits (especially the dominant one).

All of the above examples are very strong clues that the individual was raised in a double bind.

Other Effects:

The child raised in a double bind often becomes chronically depressed and may actually develop a long term, severe, emotional disturbance [25] as a result of such treatment. In our experience it is definitely a basic cause of much neurotic behavior.

Not only may the child, now an adult, exhibit chronic depression and other symptoms of emotional deprivation and abuse, but may report one or more of the following:

---

[25] ibid, [This book is worth reading in its entirety].

- Wanting to be invisible or feeling invisible.
- Doing nothing unless pushed into action by some one.
- Believing that what s/he wants as a goal is not attainable, but readily accomplishes goals set by others.
- Functioning at IQ levels below actual level.
- Chronic rebellious activity.
- Aggressiveness and belligerence towards others.
- Expecting the world to continue the same kind of double bind the parents put the child in.
- Putting others into the same double bind the child was put in; usually as a misguided form of autonomy.
- Developing chronic illness, chronic fatigue syndrome, etc.
- Survival Dependency: seriously dependent on a 'rescuer" or "care taker" in order to avoid making decisions. In milder cases, exhibiting "Decidophobia."[26]
- Paralytic Reasoning.
- Conscious and unconscious avoidance of doing anything that attracts attention for fear of having done the wrong thing, or being attacked for some reason (known or unknown).
- Fear of being happy or having things go well for extended periods of time.
- Need for some kind of ongoing problems, the fear of having no problems. Often when a problem is cleared up in one area of his or her life, another problem occurs in a different arena.
- Chronic drug use that periodically or steadily results in the individual doing poorly or becoming almost non-functional.

---

[26] Decidophobia is the fear of making decisions and often is evidenced by the individual making one great decision to have someone or some organization make his/her decisions from then on. From the book: *Learned Helplessnes,* Peterson, Maier and Seligman, Oxford University Press, Inc. 1993

- Chronic gambling with repeated losses resulting in dependency on others.
- Low self esteem.
- Fear of completing things
- Belief in unworthiness. Commonly states: "I guess I don't deserve it."
- Believes that others do not listen to or hear him/her.

Sometimes the individual may be unaware of the onset of the Belief in the double bind:

A baby, about to be born, may have hormonally signaled the mother and contractions of the uterus begin. Mother is thrilled, but because of mother's fear of the delivery, the contractions stop for some days. This registers with the unborn baby. After awhile the mother becomes fearful the baby won't be born, and the contractions begin again. This too registers with the baby.

Because the mother has a belief that causes her to be fearful of being "too happy," she allows herself only a brief moment of joy before becoming fearful that she has been "too happy."

The newly born baby has taken on a double bind as follows:

_Whatever you feel you want to happen is not supposed to occur.

_Whatever you feel you want to happen is supposed to occur.

_It is okay to have some of what you want to happen if it is accompanied by great anxiety and fear.

_If you allow yourself to become happy about what occurred or is about to occur, it will be followed by some disaster. (In this baby's case there was 3 months of colic following birth.)

In instances like this, it appears that the actual emotions of the mother are imprinted on the child. And so the child is highly vulnerable to the see-saw emotions of the mother and incorporates them as being necessary for life. In such a circumstance, the child grows into adulthood repeatedly experiencing those emotions in various situations. And, of course, the child also develops Core Beliefs to explain them: fear of success, fear of completing things, fear of being happy, being undeserving, etc.

As with all Core Beliefs, when the Core Belief in the double bind is active, the individual slips into a "trance" state and automatically follows the double bind beliefs. Thus, the individual functions at whatever age level s/he was when the belief in the double bind was established, and with the limitations of that age level.

In any given situation, once the Core Beliefs of the double bind have been established, any situation which is interpreted as starting to look like any part of the original double bind will automatically trigger the individual's original way of handling the entire double bind. Even if at the time no double bind is actually being set up.

Thus, the child, now as an adult, will unconsciously trigger the double bind Core Beliefs whenever a decision is to be made.

This will happen regardless of whether or not someone is going to tell him his decisions are good or bad at that time!

In other words: If only part one of the double bind is encountered it will trigger the reaction to the entire double bind even though no double bind is occurring. If only part two is encountered it will trigger the reaction to the entire double bind, even though no double bind is occurring. This is because the individual is "triggered" into a trance-like state by the activation of the active Core Belief: an automatic decision. (In this trance-like state, the individual thinks, feels and acts exactly as s/he *was* when the Core Belief was taken on.)

Example: Elouise was raised in a double bind imposed by her very dominant mother: "You are supposed to show me love and you are not supposed to show me love." Elouise never knew which to do, unless her mother scolded her or somehow gave her additional clues. What ever occurred, she would wait until she was criticized for her behavior in that moment and then act accordingly. Later on, when she began to go out on dates, she followed the same process. Which meant that most of her dates experienced her as cold and unfeeling. However, if her date strongly criticized her for not showing affection, she would quite avidly become very affectionate.

The original double bind becomes a self imposed, self perpetuated, self-fulfilling prophecy. Because it is so terrifying to the child, even into and throughout adulthood, the Core Beliefs regarding the response to the double bind are immediately activated whether or not any double bind is actually there. All that is required is the possible threat of the double bind awaiting them in the future. This results in the establishment of a self-fulfilling prophecy.

The child, even in adulthood, expects the world to put him/her into the double bind. Every interaction the individual has is filtered through that expectation. It doesn't even have to be actually happening with another person; it can be part of the non-verbalized thought processes of the individual, and s/he will deal with his/her own thinking as a double bind.

An example of this is Paralytic Thinking. This is a behavior in which the individual reasons him/herself into inertia.

Joseph E. Spear, D.O., Cecelia Ann Spear, M.A.

Paralytic Reasoning

Ten year old John has saved some money to buy a small tape deck. He wants his father to drive him to the store. His father says to him, "John, why don't you wait until they go on sale and you'll have saved more money and can get a better one." John has now saved more money and the tape decks go on sale. When he tells his father he is now going to get one, his father says, "John, why don't you wait a few more weeks until the new models come out. You will have saved more money and you can get the latest model with all the new features." And so it continues, and John never buys a new tape deck. John makes a decision, his father tells him to do the opposite and never agrees that John has made the right decision. But then again, Father hasn't told John that he has made a wrong decision. The double bind is in place. John believes he cannot trust his decisions and that he needs someone else there to decide for him. Let us set aside for now all the decisions John feared and avoided during his school years, that caused him to flunk out of college, that caused him to have difficulty holding jobs, and let us observe John as he reads the want ads looking for a job. As he scans the classifieds he comes across the following ad which seems perfect for him to apply for:

"Trainee wanted for men's clothing store. Work both sales and stock room. Call 555-1345."

What is John thinking about this opportunity?

"Well, let's see. If I work in the store in sales, I am going to have to wear a suit and tie. When I work in the stock room I am going to get dirty and sweaty. I am going to have to get a set of coveralls to protect my suit and tie in the stock room, but then that will cause the suit and tie to get wrinkled. That means I would have to take my suit and tie off in the stock room and change into coveralls and then I would have to take off the coveralls to change into the suit and tie. They might not have a place where I could hang my suit and tie so they wouldn't get dirty or wrinkled. If I am called back and forth between the sales floor and the stock room I won't be able to keep up and sooner or later I will get too tired and have to go home. I guess its better if I don't apply for this job."

The need to make a decision triggers John into equating it with the original double bind and the beliefs as to how to protect himself from making a decision that will result in a painful response. The Core Beliefs involved are activated and a child-like trance state is triggered and John automatically activates his usual defense. That is: to think himself into paralysis and wait for someone else to tell him what to do.

In another circumstance, John may find that he has done something on his own and performed it well. This in turn, triggers the double bind beliefs with the ensuing child-like trance state and he experiences the same miserable feelings he felt when it happened in childhood. He thought he had done something to be proud of (drawing on the wall with a crayon) and was punished for it. This means he must never allow himself to perform that well again, or make a decision and act on his own.

This may be seen in some individuals who will do something superior and then never allow themselves to do that again.

Example: Jacqueline was "tricked" into taking an art lessons.

After only three or four classes she produced a truly superior pen and ink sketch. Not only the class, but the instructor raved about the sketch. She never went back to class again. Another time she had to take tennis lessons so she could play with her husband. As part of the lessons, she was to play singles against another player. She played so superior that the Tennis Pro told her she had the possibilities of becoming a professional. She never picked up a tennis racket again. She never would go near a tennis court again.

It is important to be aware, whether it is apparent or not, that the child grows up suffering a great deal of frustration, helplessness, fear, exasperation and rage that is continued and contained at various levels of consciousness, even throughout adulthood, unless the active Core Beliefs are changed. It is also important to be aware that as upsetting and crippling as the double bind beliefs are, it is very frightening to think about no longer following them. They have become the individual's "sword and shield" in facing the world. Too, when the Core Beliefs are triggered, the individual feels exactly the same as s/he did when the original double bind was taken on. S/he temporarily shifts into being that child again with all the upsetting thoughts, feelings and reactions. This is a trance-like state that is triggered automatically. Thus the usual logical approaches are rarely, if ever, effective in ending it. The individual is helpless to change his/her behavior and thinking while the Core Belief is in action. Immediately afterwards they may berate themselves for having done something stupid.

Other Evidence of the Double Bind

One of the most common signs of the Double Bind Syndrome is a history of long term, repeated failures of self improvement attempts with or without therapy. However, it is common that there are short term improvements. What may be encountered is Survival Dependency.[27] Survival Dependency is usually encountered as a pattern of

---

[27] Survival Dependency is that dependency in which the individual believes that if s/he does not limit himself or herself, there will be nobody there to rescue or take care of him and s/he will die. Thus it is far more serious than the usual dependency, because successful improvement = death.

seemingly improving throughout the course of therapy and then "backsliding." A pattern of cycling between problem arenas such as health, love relationships, career, financial. One seems to be cleared up and another arena becomes problematical. "There is always something!"

The Way Out of the Double Bind:

The way out of the double bind is simple in theory:

Recognize that you are no longer a trapped child. You have freedom of choice.

The key factor in the resolution of the double bind is for the individual to "internally" realize that the above is true. It rarely is enough for the individual to come to that conclusion intellectually to end such a Core Belief.

Why Keep Double Bind Activity?

It is common for some of these individuals to continue the Double Bind activity because it has become an important tool.

Using such thoughts, feelings, reactions, etc. is now a tool – a means—to avoid or achieve something else. The child suffering in the double bind may discover that s/he can use it in some seemingly beneficial way. Some examples are:

- The Tyranny of the Weak: "Look how you have harmed me, now you must take care of me."
- Ways of getting love/attention: "Since I can't go to you for love, you are going to have to come to me and maybe I will show you love and maybe I won't."
- The child struggling in the double bind may come to the realization that at least s/he doesn't have to make any decisions because the parental figure doesn't expect

him/her to make good decisions and will make them for him/her.

- The child who is ignored, except when being subjected to the double bind by the parental figure, realizes that at least someone is aware of him/her when s/he is attacked for not fulfilling the double bind. In other words: "Negative attention is better than no attention at all."
- The child who feels helpless and powerless realizes that it really does pain the parental figure when the child is unable to fulfill the double bind and so uses that failure as an act of autonomy and revenge.

If there is to be complete resolution of the double bind pattern and its accompanying feelings, these "tools" must be brought out into the open and replaced with the more effective and satisfying "tools" of the mature adult.

When each of the double bind "tools" have been replaced with the more effective ways and means of the mature adult, all influence of the double bind activity should have evaporated out of the individual's life.

Symbols

The elicitation of a symbolic representation of the double bind is often very graphic as well as informative. Using hypnosis, guided imagery or similar states of consciousness, the individual is asked to allow his Non-Conscious Mind to spontaneously create a symbol representing any double binds s/he is still following.

Here are some examples of Double Bind symbols:

- A one-legged wooden chair spinning in space and I am trying to sit in it.
- A feeling that I am being pulled in two directions.
- Two adults, one on each side of a six year old child.

- Two adults dressed in clothes from the 1930's standing at the top of narrow stairs with a small child and I am trying to get up the stairs from behind them.
- A memory of my mother pushing me away and then, in front of company, wants me to come and hug her.

One of the ways of working with such symbols is to modify the symbol while still in the altered state of consciousness. We ask the individual to make an evaluation of the symbol and to upgrade it to a more appropriate symbol. For instance, the symbol of the spinning chair was comfortably shifted by the individual to an image of his walking away from the chair into a garden.

Signs Of Coming Out Of It

What is the "day to day evidence" that the double bind effects are no longer there?

1. The individual reports that setting goals and accomplishing them is effective. Surprisingly, the old blocks and failures seem to have disappeared.
2. There are increasingly fewer problems and difficulties that arise in solving problems and once solved do not return as they did in the past.
3. It seems that people in the world no longer treat the individual as the parents did in the double bind.
4. The individual no longer tries to put others in the world into the same double bind as the individual grew up with.
5. While at first, there may be some anxiety about what will happen, as the individual continues on, all such anxiety and fear disappears.

6. There are surprise experiences during which the individual has been happy or free of problems of any kind – and no disaster followed.
7. The goals the individual set at the time of the initial consultation have been, or are in the process of being, accomplished.

Elimination of the double bind and its ramifications often results in an amazing shift in the individual's life. Major patterns of limitation, fear, doubt, anxiety, loss, illness, etc. disappear to be replaced by just the opposite. Individuals frequently express astonishment at the sudden improvement in their lives.

At first, they may be somewhat anxious that such improvement will permanently disappear. If all the aspects of the double bind have been cleared and there are no other limiting Core Beliefs, the improvement is permanent.

Handling Uncomfortable Feelings

Your feelings are naturally designed to flow through you.

Your feelings and your emotional state are naturally designed to be:

1. Physically experienced, and
2. Consciously acted upon

All of your feelings are naturally designed to help. No feeling is a negative feeling or harmful feeling because each feeling is naturally designed to be experienced. You just allow it to be. You just allow the feeling/emotion to flow into whatever feelings/emotions it is going to change into until you feel empty, drained or comfortable again.

Finally you will discover that it leaves you feeling better. Suppose you are feeling guilty…you simply say to your self: "I am feeling what I think is (state the feeling)…I feel this uncomfortable feeling…in my (state whatever parts of your body you are feeling it in)…just because I am feeling this way does not mean that it is true…or false…it is just a feeling I am having…and I am just allowing myself to feel this way for now"…Perhaps after a few minutes…you discover that this uncomfortable feeling has changed…and now it feels like another uncomfortable feeling…again you say: "I am feeling what I think is (state the feeling)…I feel this uncomfortable feeling in my (state parts of body)…just because I am feeling this way does not make it true…or false…it is just an uncomfortable feeling I am having about something and I am allowing myself to feel this way for now"…Perhaps after a few minutes the feeling changes again and you say to yourself…"I am feeling what I think is (state feeling)…I feel this uncomfortable feeling in my (state body parts)…just because I feel this way doesn't mean it is true or false…it is just an uncomfortable feeling I am having about something…and I am just allowing myself to feel this way for now"…Keep doing this until you find the uncomfortable feelings have gone and the feeling you are left with is comfortable or at least neutral…If it leads you to an early event in your life…then that will be the true source of the uncomfortable feelings you are having at the time. Write them down. Somehow they will be related to the problems going on in your life now.

Chapter Five

The O'Henry Effect

O'Henry's Writings

O'Henry was best known for his short stories that developed certain concepts and feelings until close to the end of the story.

Then in the last paragraph and with a few sentences, shocked the reader by totally devastating the preceding with an outcome and emotions never suspected by the reader.

"The Lottery," a play by another author, but in the O'Henry style, is an excellent example:

Everybody is going to town. The families are from all the various farms in the area. They are going to be with their friends, show off farm-made products and every body knows, "Lottery in June, corn will come soon!"

The main dialogue is between a farmer and his wife, while his children skip along side the wagon, collecting interesting stones. Who's going to be there, what has happened with this person or that, wondering who will win the bake-off and similar conversations ensue. Everybody is at the fair. Everybody is having a wonderful time. The awards for best jelly, best cakes, etc. are given out. Then it is time for the lottery and everything quiets down.

The head of each family steps forward and pulls a token out of a hat. The winner begins to plea, "Take me, I'll go, you don't need the rest of my family!" One of the elders responds, "Now, John, you know each person in your family has to pick a token otherwise it is not a fair lottery. 'Lottery in June, corn will come soon.' You know that if we change the rules the crop may be ruined."

So, John, his wife and each of his children reach into the hat and pull out a token. And the winner is stoned to death.

As you probably just experienced to a certain extent, the ideas and emotions that you were experiencing when reading the description of what was going on, was suddenly devastated and reversed when you read the last paragraph. When such an experience is overwhelming, we call it a Sudden Traumatic Emotional Reversal or "O'Henry Effect."

Sudden Traumatic Emotional Reversal (O'Henry Effect)

A much more powerful emotional effect can occur to the young, developing child.

Picking Flowers

Consider a two year old playing alone in her back yard; fenced in, beautiful flowers, sunny day and very happy. Her mother has left her for a few minutes, and the child goes from flower to flower smelling their aromas, rolling on the soft, pleasant grass and having a marvelous time. Suddenly she sees a "pretty yellow thing on the fence." She toddles over to it and reaches for it, as she does the flowers, and it stings her! It is a wasp. Instantly, everything changes. She is stunned, shocked, in great pain, fear and turmoil. Nobody is there to explain what happened.

She has two concerns:

1. What caused this horrible constellation of feelings to occur?
2. What can she do so it never happens again?

In every case the authors have encountered, the child blames the immediately preceding feelings and emotions as the cause of the disaster.

This little girl blames her feelings of happiness, joy, autonomy and curiosity for causing such pain. She then structures a Core Belief by deciding that such feelings are to be avoided at all cost. She has decided that feeling such good feelings will only result in that horrible constellation of painful feelings again. Next time she might die. She may structure another Core Belief that she makes wrong decisions and should not act on any of her decisions unless someone tells her it is okay.

This child grows into adulthood functioning under the influence of such Core Beliefs, rather than automatically upgrading them as she becomes more experienced and knowledgeable. In fact, she consciously forgets the entire event and develops secondary Core Beliefs to explain her feelings and actions such as:

1. I don't make good decisions
2. If I am happy I will pay for it in a very unpleasant way.
3. I don't deserve to have what I want.
4. It is too dangerous to set goals and try to achieve them.

The reference memories that seem to support these Core Beliefs, may or may not include the core experience such as with the wasp. Often the individual has completely blocked this trauma from any conscious recall. This block occurs because of the tremendous emotional pain connected to the memory.

These secondary Core Beliefs, based on and reinforced by the original event, results in patterns in her life of repeated disappointment, failure, chronic low grade depression and various general emotional and physical complaints. Most of these come and go with various therapies, but are never completely eliminated.

Washing The Car

Another example is the 4 year old who observes the handy man washing the family car with a hose. He sees his father praise the handyman for doing a good job and giving him money. The child decides he has found a way to please his father and get some money, so he, too, takes the hose and proudly washes the car. The only problem is that he uses the hose on the inside of the car as well as the outside. When he proudly shows the results of his efforts to his father he is verbally and physically attacked.

He gets yelled at and painfully spanked. Thus in a single moment the pride and joy he felt on cleaning the car is turned into a constellation of horrible feelings. The child blames the pride and joy he was feeling, just prior to the attack, as being the cause of the attack, and decides to never let himself feel such feelings again.

Such feelings are a threat to his safety and survival. His father was so mad he could have killed him! And when mother say to father, "Stop it he's had enough!" and the father stops, the 4-year old begins a life long Survival Dependency. He now believes he must always have someone like the mother to protect him. If mother was happy, kind and loving he will pick someone like that as his protector/care taker/rescuer. If she was irritable, erratic and depressed, he will pick someone like that. This is covered in more detail in Chapter Eight.

Survival

The results of an "O'Henry Experience" usually change the child's beliefs about survival. The surprise attack and resulting horrible constellation of feelings are interpreted by the child as threats to his or her survival. "When you feel that way (good feelings)—something horrible happens."

There is a powerful sense that he or she would probably die if the child ever felt such a constellation of feelings again. From then on, all sorts of sacrifices are made by the child in order to avoid such a constellation of feelings – in order to stay alive.

Correction

Correction is a "re-educational process." It does this by helping the individual to correct the simplistic thinking used in childhood. It involves helping the individual to "unfold" out of the life limiting Core Beliefs into more appropriate understandings and Beliefs.

The solution is: "Do not wash the inside of the car with a hose!" – instead of the mal-adaptive solution the child originally took on. Or, as in the case of the child and the wasp – it was not that she made bad decisions – there should have been somebody there, with her, to teach her what was safe to touch and what wasn't.

The basis of re-educational process lies in the concept of:

"You are not the same person now that you were then. You never learn less! You are not the same person now that you were then...you are not the same person you were an hour ago...you are not the same person you were last week...or last month...or last year...you are not the same person you were when you were a teenager...you are not the same person you were in 1 st grade...you are not the same person you were at birth...you are not the same person you were before you were born...so why use beliefs, attitudes, thoughts, feelings, actions and reactions that were designed for a different person? If you are using beliefs, attitudes, thoughts, feelings, actions and reaction designed for a different person, then they are probably not working for you as the person you are today...so I want your Non-

Conscious Mind...to create a permanent mental storage area...that is easily accessed...at all times...by all aspects of your mind...and I want it to collect and put in there all the ways in which you are different as the person you are today...as compared to the person you were as a young, naive, developing child...it is important that your Non-Conscious Mind check out for you...and make available to you that information when ever you wish to access it...and the main reason you are not the same person now as you were back then...is that you never learn less...you never learn less...over the years...whether you realize it or not...you have been accumulating highly beneficial information, knowledge, skills, understanding about yourself and others far beyond what you may be consciously aware of...also...you are not the same person physically that you were when you were a young, naïve, developing child...thirdly, you have choices and opportunities as the person you are today...that you did not have when you were a young, naive, developing child...and all this is simply due to the fact that you have within you an inner drive to realize your entelechy...to become the highest and finest you...you can be...your body growth continued and you never learn less, so each moment of each moment you are continuing to learn...and there is much that you did as a young developing child...that you would not do today...there is much you can do today...that you could not do...as a young developing child...because you never learn less...I am not asking you to change or correct anything...but to simply allow your Non-Conscious Mind...to make you increasingly aware of all the ways you are different as the person you are now...as compared to the person you were when you were a young developing child...simply allowing your Non-Conscious Mind to so instruct and inform you...perhaps in the form of a picture or symbol...perhaps in the form of feelings...perhaps in your dreams...whatever...as you become more comfortable…during the next few moments of quiet…(You might want to make a tape recording of the above material that is double spaced and listen to it before you go to sleep.)

You are not the same person now that you were then. Fortunately, now that s/he is no longer a child, s/he has a great variety of experience and can take care of herself/himself. S/he can take care of herself/himself because "you never learn less." In other words, as you go through life you increasingly learn much more than you may consciously be aware of. For more detail about the corrective process the authors use, see Chapters Thirteen and Fourteen.

Fear Of Growing Up and the O'Henry Effect

It is common among individuals who have experienced the Triad in some degree, and particularly those who have experienced the O'Henry Effect, to have developed a belief that is a Personal Law of Survival. A Core Belief or a combination of Core Beliefs that the child then follows in a simplistic decision as to what it takes to stay alive. Among such possible decisions, the child may take on, is that it is extremely important to stay a child, regardless of how the physical body is maturing. The thinking is that if the individual, consciously and/or unconsciously "stays" a child, even though obviously in an adult body, he will not be held responsible for his decisions, and that someone else has to take care of him.[28]

Theresa

Theresa was a very lonely child, living in a commune with a highly narcissistic mother. The mother often was

---

[28] It is interesting how many of these people appear to be much younger than their chronological age.

jealous of the child's beauty. She would erratically verbally and physically attacked her. Too, by the time she was 6 years old, Theresa was regularly being sexually molested and otherwise terrified by a grandfather whom she believed was the only one who loved her. She came to believe that if she had not successfully asked for his love and attention or attracted his attention, it never would have happened. From then on she went to great effort to sabotage herself from successfully achieving whatever she wanted. At least part of her Personal Law of Survival was to not stand out unless an authority figure urged her to.

Because working in this arena did not result in resolution, a possible O'Henry Effect experience was suspected, and revealed. At age 6, her grandfather took her into a forest where there was a large pit with a fire in the bottom of it. An axe was in a nearby stump, and on which rested a sheep's head. There was a lot of blood everywhere. A somewhat large group of people stood in a circle around the pit. She had the overwhelming feeling that she should never, never tell what was happening or they would do to her what they did to the sheep.

Abreaction [29] through this event was ineffective, even the logical awareness that all those people were long since dead and could do her no harm resulted in no resolution. "There are people like that everywhere!!" In any session where this event, and others leading up to it, were discussed in hypnosis, resulted in her having nightmares for some nights afterwards, and in her financial and personal relationship becoming increasingly worse. Too, the resolution of other problem arenas in her life only seemed to make her overall personal and career situation worse.

Upon further investigation it was discovered that as another part of her Personal Law of Survival, she believed

---

[29] This is a therapeutic technique involving reliving the traumatic event and releasing the feelings associated with it.

that if she admitted she was no longer a child and that things were different now, she would lose the only means she had of getting people to insure her safety and to show her some kind of care (love).

As long as she did not think of herself as anything but a child, she believed people would help her be safe and show her some kind of care by helping her with her fears.

Therefore, it was life threatening and a potential for loss of "love" for her to show any real improvement in her overall personal life and career. It was life threatening to show any real psychological signs of being an adult. In a sense, this is a form of Survival Dependency.[30] As long as she had this Core Belief, she believed it was very dangerous for her to be happy and successful. Consequently, whenever a major therapeutic improvement occurred in other arenas, this "life saving" Core Belief would become operant and interfere accordingly.

It is important to recognize that when the individual maintains the old pattern, while stating it is too damaging in his or her daily life to try to change it; that another, very powerful Core Belief is operant. Almost invariably such a Core Belief will be powerfully grounded in Survival and/or Safety and Security.

In the above case, the Core Belief was:

"The only way I can be safe is to continue having these fears and related disasters, by functioning as a child, and then others will insure my safety. If I am happy or change my behavior, no one will be there to insure my safety and I also give up any way of getting love."

Further intervention required an approach that did not directly threaten the active Core Belief. At the same time, it was important to psychologically strengthen her. Then she could allow the shift out of the old Core Belief definition of

---

[30] Spear, J and C, "Survival Dependency," *Journal of Medical Hypnoanalysis*, July, 1996

survival into one that was more appropriate for her as an adult woman.

Such intervention must also correct the Core Belief regarding what was effective and allowable in asking for love. If the Entelechist effectively helps the individual correct one and does not also deal with the other, there is no change in the undesirable pattern.

Connie

Connie is a 45-year old woman who began having sudden panic attacks that awakened her around 4:00 a.m. These attacks would be focused on the extreme concern that she might have some terminal illness that she was unaware of.

She would go through periodic episodes of fearing cancer, cardiac disease, etc. Too, she had a history of episodes of heavy alcohol intake, frequent job changes and ongoing struggles to "save" her 22-year old daughter from whatever trouble she continuously developed.

Therapeutic intervention eventually helped her to realize, during such attacks, that these were groundless fears and she could abort the attack in a few minutes. While this is an effective coping technique, the authors prefer resolution to coping solutions. Intervention also eliminated the need for alcohol and frequent job changes.

However, every time some area of her life permanently improved, the early morning anxieties would return. Here too, a pattern was finally noted that this lady could not have a major improvement in her life without the return of her original chief complaint.

It was suspected that an O'Henry event had occurred early in life and, thus, was inquired into. Throughout her therapy there had been minor comments about her step-father, but never any traumatic event related concerning him. Investigation revealed that when, as a small child, she watched him beat her older sister to a degree that terrified her, she resolved to never do anything that would cause him to do that to her.

Since she and her sister had been happily playing just before he attacked the sister, she decided she would never be happy around him. This was to protect her and keep him from angrily killing her. This would "control" him. As she grew older, this was extended to not allowing herself to be happy other than momentarily in all situations. She had "control." She would survive.

This event was worked with and almost all the symptoms related to it disappeared. However, the anxiety attacks regarding health continued to occasionally re-appear any time she had a particularly pleasant day. One morning driving to work she had the sudden realization that she was very pleased to have such episodes. It was very pleasing to her to have the attack and then control it. That she had the power to consciously bring on the attack and to consciously stop it.

Further therapeutic intervention revealed that the above had become her working Core Belief about Autonomy. Stopping herself from being happy gave her power over her step-father. Later on, controlling the attacks with coping techniques gave her a further sense of autonomy. She was defining Autonomy as having anxiety attacks and controlling them, which in turn controlled and gave her power over her (now dead) step-father. With that revelation, the balance of her therapy was directed to gently redirecting her into more appropriate definition of Autonomy. The new Core Belief needed to be so structure in a way that would enable her to also be happy. It was important to help her release the great rage she had unconsciously developed (and consciously denied). This was done by utilizing her dreams to safely and harmlessly release her angers.

Fear of Changing

A crisis occurs at some point with such individuals when they recognize that further therapeutic investigation (with or without improvement in other arenas) results in their symptoms becoming worse. At that point they may stop therapy. Some individuals will not think to report this to the Entelechist.

Commonly, they blame financial and family problems as the causes of "not being able to continue for awhile."

The individual should understand that this is evidence of another "hidden" Core Belief and that intervention will now be aimed at accessing and correcting this through various strengthening procedures rather than what was being done, Thus enabling the individual to complete therapy. One of the most common "hidden" beliefs occurring here is the Early Multi-Stage Warning System.

Early Multi-Stage Warning System

The individual may take on the Core Belief that there must be some way of warning/stopping himself in advance so that the O'Henry event never occurs again. The individual believes that to encounter it again means death.

What does the child use to acquire such a warning system? The very same upsetting feelings s/he is trying to avoid. In some cases, a series of stages similar to the military progressive readiness stages are unconsciously developed. Commonly, this is done by setting up a multi-stage, progressive re-experiencing of the *memory* of the original, horrifying *emotions* with intensity ranging from mild and generalized to overwhelming.[31] While this will differ from individual to individual, an example might be:

Stage five: mild, vague feelings of anxiety as the individual begins to sense feelings of happiness or success or whatever the original cause was attributed to. Stage four: stronger, more definitive feelings of anxiety, perhaps bordering on a panic attack, perhaps accompanied by vague feelings of guilt and sadness. Stage three: panic attack and/or a need to hide, any of a wide range of physical symptoms such as difficulty breathing, rapid heart beat, indigestion, joint pains, headache, etc.

Stage two: the constellation of symptoms very strongly beginning to duplicate all the feelings and emotions of the memory of the O'Henry event.

Stage one: completely re-experiencing the memory of the constellation of horrifying feelings from the O'Henry event. May result in the individual suddenly freezing in place for a few moments. This might be called the "Opossum Stage" as the individual is *totally overwhelmed and may be temporarily paralyzed mentally, emotionally and physically.*

The basic purpose of this warning system is to enable the individual to survive by attempting to avoid re-experiencing completely the Sudden Traumatic Emotional Reversal. Survival is rooted in the Belief that by aborting any feeling or action that was originally credited with causing the STER in the beginning another terrible event can not occur again.

Almost invariably "being happy," "feeling good," being autonomous, curious, helpful, etc., is blamed as the cause of

---

[31] All memory is distorted and the younger the child when storing the memory, the more the distortion. The more traumatic the actual event, the more distorted the memory will be. As always, it is the memory of the trauma that is dealt with therapeutically, as there is no way of actually knowing the full truth.

the terror. Everything is designed to avoid such natural and necessary aspects of one's entelechy. By the time adulthood is reached, the real reasons the individual denies himself such natural and necessary aspects of one's entelechy is covered over with more "logical" reasons, such as: "I don't deserve it." "I'm too lazy." "God has abandoned me," etc.

There is no set group of symptoms from which to make the diagnosis other than the life pattern of the individual being fearful of being happy, having short respites from problems and suffering chronic depression in varying degrees. The problem with this Early Warning System is that while it consciously causes the individual to avoid dealing with the traumatic event, it maintains itself in every aspect of his/her life. It keeps in his/her life the very feelings that s/he does not want to experience! It "stains" every aspect because it is always there to force him to function according to early childhood decisions.

Until s/he is freed of the need for the emotional pain and discomfort s/he uses as his/her warning system, s/he is doomed to continually encounter it in almost every aspect of his/her daily life.

Any of the other symptoms of the other two legs of the Triad are supported by this O'Henry Effect.

Complete resolution of the individual's psychological problems is dependent on resolving the effects of each operant (active) "leg" of the Triad. Then the limiting Core Beliefs taken on in each arena has been either eliminated or upgraded into new, life enhancing Core Beliefs. Failure to do so insures the repeated experiencing of the undesirable patterns and reinforces a sense of being helpless to do anything about it.

In all of this, forgiveness plays an important role. This will be discussed in much more detail later on.

Handling Uncomfortable Feelings

Your feelings are naturally designed to flow through you.

Your feelings and your emotional state are naturally designed to be:

1. Physically experienced, and
2. Consciously acted upon

All your feelings are naturally designed to help. No feeling is a negative feeling or harmful feeling because each feeling is naturally designed to be experienced. You just allow it to be. You just allow the feeling/emotion to flow into whatever feelings/emotions it is going to change into until you feel empty, drained, or comfortable again.

Finally, you will discover that it leaves you feeling better. Suppose you are feeling guilty...you simply say to your self: "I am feeling what I think is (state the feeling)...I feel this uncomfortable feeling...in my (state whatever parts of your body you are feeling it in...)...just because I am feeling this way does not mean that it is true...or false...it is just a feeling I am having...and I am just allowing myself to feel this way for now"...Perhaps after a few minutes...you discover that this uncomfortable feeling has changed...and now it feels like another uncomfortable feeling...again you say: "I am feeling what I think is (state the feeling)...I feel this uncomfortable feeling in my (state parts of body)...just because I am feeling this way does not make it true...or false...it is just an uncomfortable feeling I am having about something and I am allowing myself to feel this way for now"...Perhaps after a few minutes the feeling changes again and you say to yourself..."I am feeling what I think is (state feeling)...I feel this uncomfortable feeling in my (state body parts)...just because I feel this way doesn't mean it is true or false...it is just an uncomfortable feeling I am having about something...and I am just allowing myself to feel this way for now"...Keep doing this until you find the uncomfortable feelings have gone and the feeling you are left with is comfortable or at least neutral...

If it leads you to an early event in your life...then that will be the true source of the uncomfortable feelings you are having at the time. Write them down. Somehow they will be related to the problems going on in your life now.

Chapter Six

Early Imprinting Events

Commonly these are peri-natal in timing; usually during labor and the accomplishment of the birth and the events that follow. By "peri-natal" we mean the period from conception until shortly after birth. It is not uncommon for the newborn to somehow take on the Belief that in order to be alive, it must follow the pattern of feelings experienced during it's birth or in the womb.

Janov,[32] in his work on "primal scream" and the lifelong effects of the birth experience, has noted that children may be born with a sense of struggle and win, struggle and lose,[33] etc. For example: a child delivered by caesarian section before the uterine contractions began spontaneously, may grow up believing s/he never has enough time and that s/he is always being rushed.

Here too, may lie the basic cause of Core Beliefs in the need to go through life struggling and or under pressure. This is covered in more detail in Chapter Nine.

First Stage of Bonding: Mental and Emotional Bonding Within the Womb

The "Skeletal" Structure of Pre-Natal (before birth) Core Belief Construction:

---

[32] Janov, Arthur, *Imprints*, Coward-McCann, Inc., NY, NY 1983 (This work becomes much more understandable when the reader realizes that the imprints serve as Core Beliefs – automatic decisions.)

[33] Janov, Arthur, *Primal Scream*, Perigee Books, NY, NY, 1970

It has been noted by the authors, and others, that thoughts and emotions strongly focused on by the mother, or in interactions between the mother and others around her, may be taken on as imprinted Core Beliefs by the developing fetus. That is, there is not the usual logical process as involved in formulating a Core Belief.

The fetus is imprinted with the mother's physical and emotional feelings. And usually the thoughts that accompany such feelings. The fetus may not understand the language of the thoughts, but stores them along with other input. Later on as the child learns the meaning of the words, such thoughts may have an even more powerful influence.

An unwed mother may wish her baby to be small through the pregnancy. Frequently repeating the words mentally, "Be small, baby, be small!" People ask her if she has gained some weight, but nobody realizes she is pregnant. The child is born just barely within normal size and weight As it grows older it comes to sense a second message in the phrase "be small" and that is: to not stand out or do well. And about that time begins to chew her nails down, and the inside of her mouth, as an unconscious way of making herself smaller.

Individuals in hypnosis commonly report "seeing" a powerful conflict between the mother and the father. This results in lifelong attitudes towards one or both. One individual was able to confirm with his parents the experience of his conception, the room in which it occurred, what they had been fighting over, why it did not occur in the one house he grew up in, etc. His parents were more surprised than he was.

One of the first cases the authors encountered in this regard was a 16-yr old girl who was asked in hypnosis to recall and describe "the very first Christmas tree you ever saw." At the end of the session she still had very clear memory of the tree and certain unusual ornaments on it. However, she could not recall experiencing any such tree.

When she went home and described it to her mother, her mother told her it was the Christmas tree they had while she was still in the womb.

The unborn child takes on a basic set of Core Beliefs from the mother and in some instances from those around the mother, as filtered through the mother. This is the basic set of Core Beliefs that the child operates from as it incorporates each one. The authors consider this the Primary Stage of Bonding with the mother. It is important to realize that this primary stage of bonding occurs *within* the womb. There is a tendency to credit genetic factors for some similarities, but in the authors' clinical experience, Primary Stage Bonding is the causative factor.

Limiting Core Beliefs taken on during Primary Stage Bonding may include such thoughts as:

"I have caused others pain so I deserve pain."

"I don't deserve to be happy."

"Father is a horrible person."

Beliefs of this kind almost always originate with the mother and have been automatically incorporated by the yet-to-be born baby. This is because the fetus is totally unable to differentiate between its own thoughts and feelings and those powerfully concentrated on by the mother.[34] To the unborn child they are one and the same.

Labor and Birth

Again, what the mother focuses on intently, seems to the yet-to-be-born child as it own. It automatically feels, accepts and functions using these Core Beliefs as its own.

---

[34] The authors have often wondered if this is the way the "Flee or Fight" defense is passed on from generation to generation. A learned response from the mother in the form of a Core Belief as she deals with life during the pregnancy.

Ordinarily this would be fine – if the mother has strong feelings of self worth, confidence, acceptance, love and similar life enhancing feelings throughout the pregnancy and delivery.

Then the child comes into the world with such life enhancing Core Beliefs and the accompanying feelings as an integrated part of its being on many levels. As a general rule, such individuals do not seek therapy unless something major has happened at another time.

As indicated previously, if the mother is "negatively" focused for an extended period of time or for an intense shorter period of time, the child comes into the world carrying such directives as a basic Core Beliefs structure to be automatically followed.

Many children somehow take on that such feelings are what it means to be alive and that they are supposed to repeatedly feel such feelings in order to stay alive.

The impression that we have, is that much of what is considered "genetic" or "inherited" is actually material learned from the mother in the period before and during birth.

Margie

Margie, during the course of therapy, decided to see if she could find her biological mother. She had been adopted at birth, but somehow felt it was important to discover what her biological mother was like. With a few months effort, she was able to meet with her. What she discovered shocked her.

They both were in the same profession, they both had similar temperaments, they both had the same emotional problems, etc.

She was amazed at how closely her life had duplicated her biological mother's in key areas.

This is one of many individuals who demonstrate taking on a "skeletal structure of Core Beliefs" from the mother during the pregnancy and birth process.

The authors do not see this as transmitted through the genes, because such beliefs are readily re-defined once their source is accessed. Their life patterns shift accordingly.

Second Stage of Bonding:

The bonding resulting from eye-to-eye contact with the infant at the time of birth is important, but not as powerful, nor as pervasive, as the psychological and emotional factors of the Primary Stage, and is considered, by the authors, to be the Second Stage of Bonding.

Immediately after the baby is born it may experience the most wondrous feelings of its entire life. Being picked up, held, and loved for who and what it is. These feelings are deep within the child and are released and experienced in a peaceful womb (oceanic bliss). If the mother was in turmoil, such feelings are first experienced when a tender, caring nurse took the baby to clean it up and tend to it.

The importance here is that ordinarily such feelings continue when the baby is returned to the mother. The baby experiencing the joy and love that the mother has for the baby.

If such does not occur, the baby experiences a sudden loss of the wondrous feelings and apparently, without thinking, takes on that it must repeat the feelings it had before it experienced them. Consequently, if the baby, while a fetus, was experiencing fear, guilt, anxiety, etc. from the mother, it may cyclically duplicate that pattern of miserable feelings expecting to then achieve the wondrous feelings.

If it does achieve the wondrous feelings that way, it can only keep its awareness of them for a brief time, as in its desire to continue to feel them, it again duplicates the miserable feelings.

This happens repeatedly throughout life, the child growing into adulthood unconsciously repeatedly putting itself into various events and experiences that result in the miserable feelings as an attempt to get the wondrous feelings.

Chapter Seven

Murderous Children & Lizzie Borden

Rage[35]

Lizzie Borden took an axe
Gave her mother forty whacks;
When she saw what she had done
She gave her father forty-one

Description: Lizzie Borden Rage

What else happens when a young developing child, grows up in a highly restrictive environment, severely limited by narcissistic parenting, double binds and other teachings? The the child believes s/he has to stifle himself or herself.

This results in a terrible feeling of helplessness, perhaps one of the most horrible feelings of all. As a result of such feelings, regardless of the cause, the child may develop a gradually increasing rage. This is a rage that is so powerful in the child's mind that s/he could strike out and kill the parent.

In fact, the child may have dreams or fantasies of killing or mutilating the offending parent or parents. Dreams and

---

[35] It should be noted here, that Lizzie Borden was found not guilty at her trial. The poem is quoted for the sense of childhood frustration it indicates and in no way is meant to indicate that Lizzie Borden was actually guilty.

fantasies of stabbing, crushing, beating, chopping up the offending parent or parents.

Most children, so enraged, go to great lengths to tightly control that rage. They realize it is important to not act it out and live in terror of releasing that anger. They live in terror of releasing that anger because they are afraid they will kill or greatly damage those particular individuals they are so dependent on. The parental figures they need to survive. Need to have take care of them. For to wreak physical vengeance on the parental figure(s) will result in no one to take care of them and Thus no one to supply their basic needs. Too, that others will then wreak vengeance on them. The child who actually kills the offending parent, or parents, has lost control. We hear of such reports in every generation.

The child who maintains control usually does so by great personal denial for they have already been taught not to have their own feelings, not to have their own desires, not to be who and what they really are, not to do, be or have other than what someone else has decided for them. Over and over again this message, obedience to this command is demanded; increasing the helplessness, increasing the rage and increasing the amount of energy and effort the young developing child must exert not to explode like a madman or an atomic bomb.

Those children who finally do lose control often astonish those around them because they always seemed so quiet and mild tempered, even though they raged inside.[36] And those who do not lose control, usually extend it into every aspect of their being for they realize that if they begin to feel happy they risk the loss of control; much like somebody being tickled may explode into anger when anger is the basic feeling they have been carrying around. Realizing that if they begin to release any of that tight

---

[36] See quotation at beginning of Chapter One regarding Eric.

control and allow themselves to feel other feelings, other pleasures, other desires the control is weakened, allowing them to experience that rage.

There is a powerful inner sense that such "relaxation" is dangerous. Such children, even as adults, may be very kind and mild tempered adults until they get drunk (or "pushed" in some way), and then they become terribly angry, mean, and dangerous drunks.

Once sober, they are quite apologetic. However, even something as innocuous as tickling may release a violent, angry response.

How many times has it been reported that a child was quiet and well behaved before suddenly exploding and lashing out at others?

We have used the elicitation of setting fires, bed wetting and harming animals as a guide to predict potentially violent individuals. Perhaps there is a much more accurate guide:

1. Was the message to the child: "You can not be who and what you are, you must think, feel and act the way we say."
2. "Your feelings are not valid; you do not know what you feel; I will tell you what your feelings are and what you can express."
3. How violently did the parental figures enforce such commands? How verbally and physically abusive were the parental figures when the child strayed?
4. Did the child become accident prone?
5. Did the child tend to bully other children or become a loner?

Any child growing into adulthood with one or more "legs" of the triad is potentially a violent individual if s/he loses control.

The individual described below, Joseph Kallinger, could have been saved if such criteria were applied and the home setting corrected before the age of 6.

Joseph Kallinger – The Shoemaker's Son [37]

Joe Kallinger was adopted by an older couple for the express purpose of being a servant in the house and a worker in the shoe shop. While a certain amount of lip service and effort was paid to his being their adopted son, he was treated more like a slave.

He had been told that they had rescued him from the orphanage and that he owed them for doing that. Whenever they needed to threaten his behavior, they threatened him with being sent back to the orphanage.

They were distant, unfeeling people whose only emotions towards him seemed to be criticism, anger and threats. Working in the house or the shoe shop he could see other children his age playing, laughing and having a good time. Not only was this denied him, but he was not allowed to have his own desires, his own feelings, nor state what he wanted. Due to some minor sexual actions Joseph had demonstrated at age 5, the Kallingers wanted him to be impotent, so set about conditioning him regarding his "bird." They even had a cooperative doctor pretend to do surgery on his "bird." By the time he was 6 years old he had decided he was different from everybody else. He became fascinated with knives and would threaten other children with his knife mimicking the voice of his adopted mother. He later said:

"Somehow things that were normal for everybody else are abnormal for me."

---

[37] *The Shoemaker's Son*, Flora Rheta Schreiber, Signet Books, a division of Simon and Schuster, NY.NY, 1984

When he was age 38, he and his 13-year old son were arrested for their partnership in a slaughter that occurred in 5 suburban homes over a 7-week period. But Joseph Kallinger had killed much more than that. To really get a sense of what the Triad (Chapter One) does to make a child a serial killer, it is of value to read this biography in its entirety.

More commonly, the rage is tightly controlled. The child is fearful of giving in to the helplessness and rage growing within him/her. As previously mentioned, such rage may be unconsciously turned on himself: accident-prone, getting in physical fights, or on others such as bullying other children, setting fires, torturing animals.

Being a loner, becoming a substance abuser, feeling different from others, being quiet and very careful about what one does and says are all signs that great internal control is going on – and with that, a powerful sense of helplessness and anger.

It is common for a defense attorney to state that his client was abused as a child and therefore is not responsible for his or her criminal actions. Of course this does not excuse violent physical acts, *but it gives us a sense of where to direct our efforts to reduce the influence of such a childhood environment.*

In our early work with criminal offenders, we found that the single strongest effect on reducing criminal activity was to establish strong levels of self esteem and self worth based on socially accepted concepts. Along with this comes a feeling of having a sense of autonomy in the form of peaceful applications. It is not surprising that gang membership is based on "respect." Such "respect" is based on what the gang values, which is often quite the opposite of those of society.

The solution of course, is for the individual to realize and understand that things are different now. That s/he is no longer a young, naïve, helpless child trapped in a terrible situation, even thought they may feel that way much of the time. Back then, they were enraged and had no choice, no means of escape, no real way to exercise their autonomy, as they do now. Now they do not have to keep such feelings of helplessness and rage in order to protect themselves and protect others. Back then, it was important to restrict themselves and their feelings as they have over the years.

But things are different now, and the helplessness they had then no longer exists. It no longer exists because they are not a trapped child. They have choices, powers, abilities, alternatives that they did not have then. It is important for them to realize not only intellectually, but "internally," that they did a marvelous job controlling themselves. They fought the battles and won the war deep within themselves. Now it is time to realize that after winning the war, comes peace.

The "Limiting Triad" consists of three "Legs," any one of which can cause the kind of rage we are talking about:

1. Narcissistic Parenting—the greatly self-centered parent who is only concerned with his/her feelings and life and what the child can do for this parent. This is what we call the "Queen" form. The "Stage Mother," which most everyone is familiar with, and the "Attacker," who attacks any thing the child does seemingly better than the parent. The Attacker may attack indirectly or directly but the results of all are the same.
2. Double Bind—where the child is given directly opposing orders/expectations and has to fulfill both. The child of course, has no escape as s/he would if an adult.
3. Sudden Traumatic Emotional Reversal (O'Henry Experience)—where the child is happily playing or doing something and is suddenly and overwhelmingly attacked by someone or something and blames being curious, happy, etc. for the cause of the attack, and

resolves to never let herself or himself feel that way again. In each of the three legs of the Triad, the child is learning to not be real. S/he can not have his or her own feelings. S/he can not have his or her own goals. S/he can not express himself or herself truthfully. S/he must hide who and what s/he really is in order to fit in with the demands of the parental figure(s). This, at first, results in feelings of helplessness which soon becomes anger.

There is no resolution. As the child continues to live in such a suppressive environment, the anger continues to grow and becomes a rage.

S/he may have thoughts of killing or harming the parental figure(s) in some way. If s/he loses control of the rage behind these thoughts, s/he may actually try to harm the parental figure(s), just as Lizzie Borden was accused of doing.

Fortunately, most children growing up in these circumstances do not directly strike out. They withdraw as much as possible. They anesthetize themselves with depression. They know they must not strike out for it would mean great harm to those they are most dependent upon for survival. Therefore, to so follow through would result in the child's death or great disaster.

So the child takes on a multi-dimensional "tension" to control the rage. S/he may turn it on herself/himself: becoming accident-prone, carving on her/his body with a razor blade, are among the more common. S/he may so suppress the anger that s/he is consciously totally unaware that it is even smoldering within her/him. Even in work in altered states, in may be rigidly hidden and at first not seem to be there. The child, now an adult, has come to believe s/he must maintain the "tension." To not have that special "Tension" threatens his/her survival (according to his/her beliefs). Thus the child can not allow any feeling that may "relax" that control, such as being happy, loving, or joyful for extended periods of time, feelings of being safe, etc.

Since s/he is no longer trapped and living with the parental figure(s), there is no real reason to maintain the "tension," but that logic cannot release her/him—yet.

Unconsciously, her/his mind works to maintain the "tension": "back engineering," so to speak, by unconsciously setting up events and experiences and attitudes where s/he feels helpless and angry. Thus as an adult, s/he still can not allow herself/himself to be truly happy for extended periods of time, cannot have extended periods of a problem-free life, cannot be into a fully relaxed and loving relationship, etc.

The solution lies in:

1. accessing and releasing the anger, safely and harmlessly in dreams and,
2. a process of forgiveness.

Correction involves the individual becoming emotionally neutral to the events and individuals that caused him to feel so helpless and angry. Forgiveness is a powerful means of doing so.

Forgiveness

Ideal forgiveness would be to the extent that "it never happened, it was just a bad dream." This is not a process of denial. If anything, it is just the opposite. It is a process of accepting that what is past is only memory now, and making a conscious decision to forgive. Recollecting that one of the meanings of "forgive" is "to let go."

Failure to forgive is to sentence oneself to a lifetime of repeated episodes of unhappiness, emotional turmoil and a variety of limitations in what the individual denies himself or herself by choosing to not "let go." Many individuals, in therapy, were asked what would happen in their lives if they completely let go and forgave. Their responses were uniformly those describing a better, happier, healthier life.

"Perfect" forgiveness would be to feel the same way you would have felt "if it had never happened." Thus, the individual accepts the event, but chooses to remember it and react to it in a fully neutral way. To react to the memory as though it never happened.

> *"The next best is that the individual is freely, unhesitatingly and completely able to wish the other well, understanding that this does not mean the other person was right or s/he was wrong or that s/he will allow others to treat him/her that way again." Anon.*

Handling Uncomfortable Feelings

Your feelings are naturally designed to flow through you.

Your feelings and your emotional state are naturally designed to be:

1. Physically experienced, and
2. Consciously acted upon

All your feelings are naturally designed to help. No feeling is a negative feeling or harmful feeling because each feeling is naturally designed to be experienced. You just allow it to be. You just allow the feeling/emotion to flow into whatever feelings/emotions it is going to change into until you feel empty, drained or comfortable again.

Finally you will discover that it leaves you feeling better. Suppose you are feeling guilty…you simply say to your self: "I am feeling what I think is (state the feeling)…I feel this uncomfortable feeling…in my (state whatever parts of your body you are feeling it in…)…just because I am feeling this way does not mean that it is true…or false…it is just a feeling I am having…and I am just allowing myself to feel this way for now"…Perhaps after a few minutes…you discover that this uncomfortable feeling has changed…and now it feels like another uncomfortable feeling…again you say: "I am feeling what I think is (state the feeling)…I feel this uncomfortable feeling in my (state parts of body)…just because I am feeling this way does not make it true…or false…it is just an uncomfortable feeling I am having about something and I am allowing myself to feel this way for now"…Perhaps after a few minutes the feeling changes again and you say to yourself…"I am feeling what I think is (state feeling)…I feel this uncomfortable feeling in my (state body parts)…just because I feel this way doesn't mean it is true or false…it is just an uncomfortable feeling I am having about something…and I am just allowing myself to feel this way for now"…Keep doing this until you find the uncomfortable feelings have gone and the feeling you are left with is comfortable or at least neutral.

If it leads you to an early event in your life…then that will be the true source of the uncomfortable feelings you are having at the time. Write them down. Somehow they will be related to the problems going on in your life now.

Joseph E. Spear, D.O., Cecelia Ann Spear, M.A.

Chapter Eight

Survival Dependency[38]

Plagued with having to be "unreal." Attacked for any expression of who or what he or she is. Belittled for any decision that doesn't fit with the dominant parental figure's wishes. The child has to find some way to survive.

It doesn't take long for many such children to come to the conclusion that they do not make good decisions and it is better to get someone else to make decisions for them.

Sometimes the individual will make a major decision to avoid making major decisions in the future: join the armed forces, become a monk, get married, join a cult, and the most common one – get people to rescue you.

The Need to Have Problems

One of the more common ways is to always have some sort of a problem. When one is clearing up, another one is waiting at the door. School problems, health problems, money problems, car problems, emotional problems, job problems, love problems and on and on. Often cycling over and over again.

Such people cannot conceive of a world in which they are basically free of problems. To them it is like living on another planet! In a sense they see this as perfectly normal: "Having problems is just the way life is. Everybody has problems!" One of the most crippling and exasperating ways of surviving is what we call "Survival Dependency."

---

[38] Modified from the form as published in *Journal of Medical Hypnoanalysis*, July, 1996

Survival Dependency Defined:

- A malignant form of dependency that is differentiated from the usual forms of neurotic dependency, by the powerful belief that the individual must stay dependent and severely limit any kind of self improvement or he will die. This results in the individual functioning within a very narrow range in almost all aspects of his life. The usual therapeutic approaches are at best only temporarily effective and, at worse, cause further damage.

Introduction

Survival dependency is a very malignant form of dependency. Because of its basic structure, it corrupts every aspect of the individual's life. It strongly equates staying alive with having someone to be dependent upon, to the extent that <u>such an individual can not allow himself to improve and develop beyond a narrow range</u>.

It is characterized by:

1. An early event or series of events that are perceived as life threatening or potentially life threatening.
2. The intervention, direct or implied, of an individual who is perceived as a Protector/Rescuer/Caretaker.
3. The Core Belief that any show of independence or individual capability beyond a narrow range will result in loss of the Protector/Rescuer/Caretaker and surely result in death.

Protector/Rescuer/Caretaker

The Protector/Rescuer/Caretaker is usually symbolic of a particular parent or parental figure. This is the individual that the Survival Dependent believes must be there in order for him to stay alive. There must always be a Protector/Rescuer/Caretaker at hand, otherwise the Survival Dependent becomes anxious and eventually panics until a Protector/Rescuer/Caretaker is again at hand.

The Survival Dependent often duplicates the Protector/Rescuer/Caretaker with someone at home, work, school and in other situations. Some times this is seen in the form of symbolically re-creating the family using co-workers, fellow students or people frequently socialized with. In such a circumstance at work for example, the supervisor may be seen as parental, co-workers as various siblings and other workers as other members of the family.

With some adults, it can be a friend who is consulted with daily. However this does not necessarily indicate Survival Dependency.

It is common for two people with this problem to live together, alternating roles of Protector/Rescuer/Caretaker and Survival Dependent! "Ping-Pong Dependency." In such an instance, if either one begins to improve and really do much better, this becomes a threat to the other party who immediately tries to restore the arrangement with various threats or actions.

Zelda

Zelda grew up in a family that fled Europe just after the Second World War. Her father and mother had escaped with the utmost difficulty, encountering many dangers and using their wits to survive. They taught Zelda that life "out there" was dangerous. They taught her to be very concerned about "others." She came to believe that unless they were with her, she could be seriously harmed. As she grew older and was expected to go to school on her own, some of her experiences with other children eased off those fears. She began to become more open, happier and started inviting other children over to play in her yard. Her father, who was unnerved by any emotion other than seriousness, beat her in front of the other children and ran them off. She took on that if she did what she wanted, if she was happy, she would be attacked. She could never really get what she wanted and keep it, or she would be attack. It would be necessary to always have someone there to decide for her. To direct her.

Zelda was terrorized by the actions of her father. Despite the terror, s/he came to believe that she actually needed someone to tell her what to do in order to avoid his attacks. She came to believe that she needed *that* parent to tell her how to be, act, think and feel in the world. Her father was afraid to face the world directly. He had escaped from Europe by being invisible, not drawing attention to himself, being fearful of every possibility. So beginning around the age of 9, he would have her do certain things for him. He would tell her exactly what to say, who to say it to and how to do it – because he was afraid to do it himself. When she didn't do as he told her to he would become enraged and beat her. If it didn't work out the way he wanted it to, he would become enraged and beat her. And throughout the beatings telling her it was all her fault. She came to believe she did not make good decisions and always had to have someone around to tell her what to do. And so Zelda became a Survival Dependent.

Causes:

To date the following precipitating events have been encountered:

1. Rescued from a terrifying parent by the other parent during an event where the child believes s/he is about to be seriously damaged or killed. This could be simply a very angry parent who yells and screams terrifyingly.

2. Indoctrination by a fearful parent who raises the child to believe s/he cannot survive without the parent nearby. Remember the fearful mother whose child was not allowed outdoors alone until age 7?

3. Indoctrination by parental figures who scares the child into believing that s/he makes wrong decisions that could result in the child being seriously damaged or killed if someone else doesn't make the decisions for the child.

4. Life-threatening accident during which individual takes on the belief that s/he cannot survive without being institutionalized or taken care of by someone else. Currently this one seems to be preceded by family history of cruel or uncaring parents.

5. Belief that chaos results in survival because someone came into the chaos to save the individual.

6. Event in which child comes to believe that being in a particular crises enabled it to survive by being rescued or protected from the crises. Therefore, for the rest of its life it must have cycles of crises in order to continue living. Generally #5 and #6 are a Belief that "to feel safe is dangerous, and to feel unsafe is safer." Thus: "If I want to feel safe, I must not feel safe because feeling safe is dangerous. If I feel unsafe, then I will feel more safe, because not feeling safe is safer."

It is important to be aware that the experiencing of any of the above does not automatically result in survival dependency. The Core Belief must be taken on that being alone means death and one must limit oneself so as not to appear too capable or successful or happy and Thus lose the Protector/Rescuer/Caretaker. <u>Thus, improving one's self is a death defying act!</u>

Using the Beast As Protection From the Beast

On occasion, an unusual aspect of the Protector/Rescuer/Caretaker – Survivor Dependent interaction is the evolving into using the very person one is terrified of, to protect you – from them. This is like a lamb using the wolf that is trying to eat it, to protect itself from that wolf and the rest of the world.

The child may be terrified of the parent and yet come to believe that they need that parent to protect them in some way.

Zelda

You remember Zelda. She needed protection from her father, yet she believed he was the only one that could decide for her. The father believed he could not survive without her to perform in his place. He beat her in front of other children, embarrassed her when she was with others; he wanted to her isolate her so she could take care of his needs.

Not only was there a "ping-pong" dependency, but Zelda's protector from her father, was her father. "I needed protection from him and the world. I needed to be told how to be and what to do. I did not know who, or how, I was supposed to be out there. My father told me how to define myself, and how to be out in the world. He told me what dangers to look out for; how to avoid them; what to do if they occurred. So I needed him to be my protector."

Daniel

Daniel too, was terrorized by his father. "My father never instructed me as to how to do what he ordered, I was just supposed to know. When I failed to do it right he would go into a rage and then finish the chore for me. I needed protection from him, and yet I needed him to successfully complete things for me."

119

Susan

Susan's father had enough of her alcoholic mother and left the family. At first, Susan was quite pleased. Now that he was gone, so too, was his self centered behavior and the double binds he would put her in.

However, shortly after he left, she realized that her drunken mother could not take care of her. She struggled to take care of them both all the while feeling angry, guilty, helpless, inadequate and other similar feelings. She unconsciously moved into Survival Dependency. She had come to the decision she could not do what was required by herself. She had to rely on her father to come by from time to time to save them. Now she was dependent on the very person she was most fearful of. Like the others, the Protector/Rescuer/Caretakers she kept in her life, resembled her father in key ways. "I'm dating a new man who happily treats me well – however he has my father's remoteness."

Bach and Goldberg[39] call them "crazy makers":

"Even though 'crazymaking' ultimately proves very destructive to its victims, causing extreme detachment, instability, over dependency, chronic anxiety and even breakdown, the victim's poor self-image and deep feelings of inadequacy tend to cause him to cling to the 'crazymaking' relationship and view it as a critical, life-sustaining involvement. Such a relationship of hate disguised by love is all the victim feels he is worth."…

"The victims have learned to be frightened and overwhelmed by the 'cruel, evil world' outside, and the 'crazymaking' relationship, destructive as it is, seems safer and more secure than the uncertainties of the 'real' world out there."…"The 'crazymaking' relationship is an exhausting one, physically and emotionally…one of chronic

---

[39] Bach, G. R. and Goldberg, H, *Creative Aggression*, Doubleday and Co, Garden City, NY, 1974 pg.92

oscillations, unpredictability, manipulative-ness, confusing messages and (double) bindings. The only way out for the victim may be a total emotional breakdown, physical illness or a violent outburst. Even in short encounters with crazymakers, one may find oneself wishing to run away, feeling fatigued, reaching for cigarettes or alcohol, becoming headachy or escaping into sleep."

Consider a European child brought to this country soon after the end of WWII. The parents having escaped the Germans, the bombings and the Russians. Such parents are highly suspicious and guarded. They have learned to watch out for potential danger in every direction and from every person. Too, they must learn to speak English and survive in this country.

The child learns the new language more rapidly and is less tense and suspicious about being out in the world and learning more about the new country. The father believes he must tightly control her. She is to make no friendships and she is to be exactly where he wants her to be all the time. He holds her out in front of him as his tiny agent. She is to translate what is said. She is to speak for him, and heaven help her if it doesn't work out because then she is to blame, even though she may be only 8 or 10 years old. This parent must keep her restricted and nearby because he feels fearful and inadequate. His rages and punishments strike great terror in her. Yet she believes she doesn't know her identity until he defines it for her. She doesn't know how to deal with the world each day, until he tells her how to. By the time she has reached her early twenties, she has had two "nervous breakdowns" and by the time she is 40 she is on welfare, even though she previously demonstrated skills that led to her taking over his job in a company that he was fired from. After a year passed, he did every thing he could to undermine her, in that job and in her confidence level; eventually she was fired.

Louise

A similar dependency was set up by Louise who's father molested her when she was a toddler. Of course this felt good to her because her anatomy was designed to respond that way. Other than that, the father was frightening and frequently erratic. Being very wealthy, he used his wealth to control the family.

One day he hurt her and she became very fearful of him and at the same time wanted him to hold her and love her. She could not allow him close and would run off screaming. After that there were times he brutally tried to get her to come close and not be afraid of him. He would grab her arm, pull her hair, etc. A rather strange way of trying to get her confidence.

Nonetheless, she still wanted him to hold her, and so she took on a Core Belief that she would function within the range we call "Survival Dependency" to get money from him. The hope was that somehow by maintaining this dependency, sooner or later he would show her love or, at least, that he cared about her.

Consequently, she took on the Core Belief that if she had money she had no control. Her personal myth was in the form of a Core Belief that said, "If I have no money, I have control." This was because she had began a process, as a young child, to control the father by needing money.

False Independence in a Survival Dependent

When a younger child comes into the situation, the Survival Dependent child may suddenly become very capable for an extended period of time.

Kathryn

Consider Kathryn, who discovered that she couldn't compete with the new baby in the house by being dependent, so she chose to become an overachiever. The Belief was that by doing what the parents want (being successful in school, extra-curricular activities, etc.) the parents will keep taking care of her. Somehow she would get a lot more attention, just like the baby.

She maintained a very capable, high level of functioning in school and extra-curricular activities for many years. Around the age of 16 she realized she was going to be expected to move into adulthood and take care of herself. At this point she stopped what she was doing and over a few months regressed to the dependent thinking and behavior she had about the time her sister was born.

Symptoms

Usually most of the following patterns:

1. Repeated problems in life
    - As soon as one problem is resolved than another problem takes its place.
    - Makes decisions that are designed to solve current problems but which result in more problems now or later. (Maladaptive Solutions)
    - No, or a rare, history of being basically happy for extended periods of time.
    - Consistently will have someone (parental figure) who is fulfilling the role of Defender/Rescuer/Protector/Caretaker.
    - Exhibits rage towards self and/or the one depended upon.
    - May be passive aggressive dependent personality.

- May be a highly demanding dependent, as in the case of a woman with severe obesity and arthritis. She sat like a queen in her bed making demands on all in the family and upon her doctors; raging when they didn't perform as she expected. Which was never, because her beliefs wouldn't allow her to be satisfied with their efforts or level of concern for her.
- Focusing on the concept that being without problems causes great apprehension or outright fear.
- May report highly chaotic life
- May report life of repeated crises
- May feel like he or she has been either cursed or abandoned by God.
- May believe that he or she is being tested by God, much like Job was biblically.

2. Never being basically happy for more than short periods of time.
   a. Being happy seems frightening, alien and impossible. "Another World!"
   b. May state that whenever s/he has been happy the individual has had to "pay for it" afterwards as it was followed by some disaster. (Monkey's Paw Syndrome)[40]

3. Frequent illnesses or history of chronic illness.
   These may range from chronic minor skin irritations to being accident prone to developing a very serious organic disease.

4. Always has someone whom they consciously or unconsciously depend upon. Never really without someone there for them. Loss of one person is immediately replaced by another person, often before the first one has left. As one woman said, "I have one lover on my lap, another going out the door and a third

---

[40] Poe, Edgar Allen, *The Monkey's Paw*

waiting in the wings." While the Survival Dependent consciously yearns for independence and individual success, such states mean "being alone," and that means death.

5. Has double binds in childhood.
6. Fear of being alone.

Anything which threatens the presence of the Protector/Rescuer/Caretaker results in a range of emotions from simple anxiety to full blown terror if the Protector/Rescuer/Caretaker leaves without there being a replacement. Such individuals may be mistakenly treated for panic attacks and agoraphobia, but the real problem lies in Survival Dependency, of which these states are simply symptoms. The symptoms are "tools" to prevent being alone.

7. Fear of being independent/successful.

Unless specifically encouraged to do so by the Protector/Rescuer/Caretaker. Usually the Survival Dependent will actively pursue accomplishing what the Protector/Caretaker indicates unless it would result in too much independence and Thus threaten the loss of the Protector/Rescuer/Caretaker. Since the Protector/Rescuer/Caretaker has his or her own Core Beliefs about needing someone to take care of, the Protector/Rescuer/Caretaker may contribute consciously or unconsciously to maintaining a double bind. A child with a talent for music may be strongly encouraged to develop that talent by the narcissistic parent, who also attacks him for not doing very well and then accuses him of being big-headed when he wins a music award.

8. History of being in therapy for long periods of time with little or no improvement.

Where improvement has occurred it seems to be short lived. The Entelechist finds that these individuals seem to clear up one problem area only to have it replaced by another. It is common for them to have problems in alternating arenas: physical, financial, work, school, relationships, therapy, and so on, and so on, and so on.

The all-pervading factor is SURVIVAL: staying alive by always having an appropriate Protector/Rescuer/Caretaker to depend upon.

Survival Dependents encounter great fear at the thought of allowing themselves to start:

- doing better
- thinking well of themselves
- being healthier
- being successful
- being happier
- having fewer problems
- acting on one's own
- being alone and/or independent

Differs from other neurotic dependency as popularized:

Cinderella Syndrome:[41] Independent until involved with someone else emotionally, then totally surrenders all decision making over to the "significant other." Often highly successful when not emotionally involved with a significant other.

Earth Mother Syndrome:[42] This is a condition where the male has come to believe that the female loves him, because he is emotional and dependent on her. She has come to represent the mother he lost, or the mother he never had. It

---

[41] *Cinderella Syndrome: Women Who Fear Independence*, Colette Dowling, Summit Books, NY, NY, 1981
[42] *Hazards of Being Male*, Herb Goldberg, Ph.D., New American Library, Bergenfield, NJ

results in increasing dependency and emotional expressions of all kinds. It is usually readily reversed by pointing out the syndrome to the male while in an altered state of consciousness (ASC). The male is then reminded that the female became attracted to him for certain reasons and never meant to encourage him to become an overgrown, helpless child. Compared to the Survival Dependent who has great fear about not staying within the "box," this male often moves very rapidly out of Earth Mother Syndrome.

Specific Need Satisfied: Here dependency is utilized to get a particular need satisfied such as the earlier example concerning love. It is not considered a life or death matter but simply related to the particular instinctoid need.[43] The Survival Dependent sees any improvement as threatening his continued existence.

Differentiating From Other Dependency:

It differs from other forms of dependency in that it is constantly and consistently distorting every aspect of the individual's life that underline threatens to improve the individual because such improvement is seen as causing the loss of a Protector/Rescuer/Caretaker and Thus will result in death.

Questions Indicating Survival Dependency:

1. As you look over your life has there been extended periods of time that you have been basically happy?

---

[43] The authors modification of Maslow's Instinctoid Needs in [our] order of importance: 1. Autonomy, 2. Survival, 3. Safety and Security, 4. Acceptance and Belonging, 5. Love: giving and receiving, including sex, 6. Self Worth, 7. Spiritual Grounding.

2. As you look over your life have there been <u>extended</u> periods of time in which you have been basically free of any problems?
3. As you look over your life have there been <u>extended</u> periods of time in which you have been free of physical symptoms and in good health?
4. As you look over your life have there been <u>extended</u> periods of time in which you were comfortably alone, that is, not closely involved with someone on a day to day basis?
5. As you look over your life have there been <u>extended</u> periods of time in which you have been successful?
6. As you look over your life is there a pattern of struggling to improve or do better in some area of your life and as that begins to improve something else gets worse or a new problem arises?
7. As you think about it, is it scary to think about being completely on your own—no one waiting in the wings to help you or be with you in some way?

The individual with Survival Dependency will answer "no" to most of the questions #1 through 5 and "Yes" to #6 and 7.

Sometimes Survival Dependency is disguised. Like a physical cancer, a high degree of suspicion is required, especially where there is a repeated pattern of improvement loss of improvement. Too, one person's level of success may be another person's bottom line for failure.

The key factor is that there is always someone else available:

someone to talk to every day or so, chronic illness, only involved in team work, etc.

If you think you maybe a Survival Dependent but have some doubt, ask yourself:

"If I had never had any more major problems does that somehow seem to be impossible for me? Like living in a foreign world or being on another planet?"

An individual may come to believe that the only way his father has of showing him love is to give him material gifts such as money. This individual may come to believe, early in life, that the way to show he loves his father is to make himself needy.

His father now has frequent reasons to give him money and other material things.

Thus, a type of dependency occurs, in which the son constantly and consistently is dependent upon the father or a father figure to bail him out financially. Usually this fits in with the parental beliefs about showing "love." This is not a Survival Dependent. It is a life limiting Core Belief designed to give and receive love.

In the period before becoming a Survival Dependent, the child is in a very painful situation. It seems life threatening to him (even if it is not). Another person (usually a parental figure) intervenes and the child takes on the Belief that he has to be in trouble if he is going to survive.

Example: A 4-year old girl is being beaten by her father and he is chasing her around the house. She is terrified because when he beats her he makes her take as much of the pain as she can without crying out. In the past this has caused her to eventually pass out during such beatings. This time she has decided to try to escape the beating by running away. As she eludes him he becomes angrier and more threatening. Now she is really terrified because she knows he has the power to kill her if he finally catches her. He does catch her and starts beating her, but this time her mother intervenes and tells him to stop. To the child's surprise he does stop.

At this time the child takes on the belief that in order to survive, in order to continue to live, she must be in a position that someone is always there to defend her.

She must be in circumstances that requires someone to be there to rescue or save her. To this little girl the ways and means of doing this is obvious: if she is being threatened by someone, if she is in serious trouble, mother or someone like mother will then always be there to defend her.

As she grows older this becomes expanded, by using asthma and other illness' so that "mother" is always attendant. As she continues to mature she enlarges the Belief into the fear of being happy and the fear of having no problems because she has come to believe that in order to survive, in order to not die, she must constantly have some sort of problem or chaos going on. Thus, she can not be happy for fear this will result in mother or a mother figure seeing that everything is all right, and she does not need her standing by.

The 41-year old woman I am speaking of has had at least one major physical, emotional, marital, or legal disaster happening every two years since age 4!

This highly malignant form of dependency results in a pattern of attacking oneself in order to cause someone else to standby to defend or rescue the individual.

"If I attack myself, someone will see that I am in trouble and rescue me and I will continue to live."

One woman believed that she had to be at the breaking point – practically at death's door before her mother would rescue her from a psychotic father. Consequently she had a pattern of gradually increasing disasters and chaos until finally she was suicidal or near bankruptcy or getting drunk regularly and then her mother would help her.

The individual trying to survive by such dependency can not let himself or herself even begin to do well and so may develop additional symptoms of the passive aggressive personality. Usually a long term smoldering anger develops over the years:

1. Because of the belief that the Survival Dependent must repress his talents and abilities both consciously and unconsciously, and
2. at the Protector/Caretaker, because of the helplessness and fear that the other person cannot live up to the Survival Dependent's expectations.

It is important to be aware that one of the most frequent causes of Survival Dependency is the double bind.

Fear of Growing Up

Connected with this is the fear of growing up or the fear of not staying a child.

The Survival Dependent cannot be an adult because that would mean s/he would not need care or protection and would be abandoned and die. And so, as the body matures, the Survival Dependent is disconcerted by any evidence that adulthood is eminent, i.e.: onset of secondary sexual characteristics, menses, etc. A kind of deliberate delusion occurs in which this person may consciously state they are an adult, but the belief system is that they are still a child, regardless of what the physical body is doing. Of course, the rest of the world sees an adult acting childishly. This individual must maintain a self-inflicted illusion that s/he is a child, despite all the physical evidence to the contrary.

Subcategories of Survival Dependency

As of this writing, it appears that there are at least three sub-categories involving other instinctoid needs along with survival.

1. Love
2. Safety and Security
3. Both of the above

Survival Dependency and Love

An individual may have come to believe that by being dependent, s/he achieves "love." Such "love" is actually another word for survival. Actually, the working definition of love, in this case, is usually based on how "parenting" is defined, rather than on adult expressions and experiences of love. What the child experienced as "love," was actually the parental ways of raising the child. Ordinarily, there would be a great deal of love involved. With narcissistic parents, there is very little.

Survival Dependency and Safety

In other instances, it may be based on staying safe and secure. As long as the Survival Dependent has its Protector/Care taker, it is safe and secure.

To date, all other formats seem to be variations of one or both of the above subcategories.

Survival Dependency, Love and Safety

It is not uncommon for both to be present and each one needs be dealt with individually. This has been determined by working in one category with the individual; the individual feels much better for several hours or days, and then reports the problem has returned. In truth it has not returned, it is simply the activity of another Core Belief maintaining the Survival Dependent pattern. The basis of this must be elicited and then specifically worked with.

It should be remembered, that trying to correct Survival Dependency using the Logical Mind is worse than a waste of time, because it triggers additional activity of the limiting Core Beliefs involved. As long as one or more of those Core Beliefs is in place, improvement means death. Any attempt to correct these beliefs logically simply activates the Core Belief that to do so will result in death.

Daniel

So terrified of his father, Daniel discovered that he had to have his mother there to somehow protect him. Even though she too, was terrified of her husband.

So at this point, we aimed our corrections of his Survival Dependency from the standpoint of safety and security. He felt wonderful, and things went really smooth for several days and then the old feelings began to come back. This time it was discovered that being a Survival Dependent was designed to achieve love in the form of parenting. Needless to say, this came as no surprise as his wife. Again for a few days things went really well. He felt like he was cured. And then the uncomfortable feelings began to come back. This time it was elicited that as terrified as he was of his father, he had come to believe that he need his father there to correct his mistakes and then he could succeed (sort of...).

Remember, his father never told him the right way to do what was expected of him, and so he never did it right. His father became furious, punished him and did the chore as he wanted it done. (This, of course, is hiring the wolf to protect the lamb from the wolf and the world.) As long Daniel stayed a Survival Dependent, someone would be there to do it correctly and help his success. Again he felt wonderful for almost a week and then the feelings returned.

This time we elicited that he would be disloyal to his mother if he went on to be happy and successful. The two of them would cower somewhere in fear of his father. He saw them as "kindred spirits." They were an alliance against a common danger. If he went on to be confident, successful, etc., all the things his mother had said she wished she could be, this would be abandoning her. He would then feel guilty and would revert to Survival Dependency. This might be considered a form of Acceptance and Belonging connected to being a Survival Dependent.

Note, that simply dealing with Survival Dependency in a general manner was not adequate to get the correction. It had to be dealt with in each of the subcategories it was actively a part of.

So there is, at least, one very powerful arena that the Survival Dependency is structured on. It also "spills" over into the other instinctoid needs. It quickly became apparent that even though the individual feels better and has his/her life temporarily improve over a few days, return of the feelings and pattern indicates the "swamp" from which it springs, has not been drained.

So at least one, and maybe more, of the Instinctoid Needs is individually connected to Survival Dependency. So far, the example of Daniel demonstrates what has been discovered to date. Love, Safety and Security, Acceptance and Belonging, Success; each one that is operant must be dealt with at the same time we are working with Survival Dependency, otherwise it is unlikely the connection is made and corrected by the Non-Conscious Mind.

Blaming Vs. Guilt

It is usually quite easy to learn that guilt is present. The individual will frequently admit to guilt with hardly any hesitation at all. However, while guilt may be associated with Survival Dependency, "blaming" is a major factor.

The most common scenario, to date is, the child growing up in an environment of constantly being blamed or criticized. Sometimes the offending parent tries to sugar coat it by telling the child s/he is acting as the "devil's advocate." Such a child may develop into being a "blamer." They may become hypercritical, nagging, easily enraged individuals. They may be totally, consciously unaware that the blaming they experienced while growing up has caused them to shift into Survival Dependency. Not only becoming dependent, but copying the offending parent in this respect because that seems to be the expression of power. If the other parent, or a parental figure, rescues the child from an attack of blaming, or repeated attacks of blaming, it is a simple step to come to believe that somebody has to be there now, and in the future, to continue such protection.

Shifting Out of Survival Dependency

Therapeutic intervention is required to shift the individual out of Survival Dependency. This is because the very nature of Survival Dependency consistently results in the dependent person unconsciously doing things in such a manner that the dependency is maintained – especially when it looks like the problem has been solved. Any intervention must be designed to be effective without pushing the individual to "improve" or "do better." Consequently, self-help programs have a history of short-lived success for this individual.

Re-defining must be aimed at helping the individual to unfold out of Survival Dependency rather than "getting better." If the Core Experience (CREX) that resulted in this belief occurred about 6 years of age or younger, logical dissection and analysis of the Belief System usually will not result in any improvement. What is more effective is to have the individual's Non-Conscious Mind (which is everything that is not the Logical Mind), make the correction. Then repeatedly go through the same process at least once each session for several sessions. If the onset is after 6 years of age, the individual may move out of Survival Dependency via a logical approach while in a trance state.

Remember: it is very important not to encourage these individuals to get better or improve but rather to have the "Non-Conscious Mind" make the appropriate decisions and Thus the individual <u>unfolds</u> into maturity and capability – without any Logical effort. This process is discussed in more detail in Chapter 13.

If the root of the survival dependency is the Double Bind, the individual may not make any real changes even though the Entelechist skillfully deals with the dependency. In such a case, the Entelechist must help the individual free himself from the Double Bind.

In practice, the double bind may be quite readily apparent at the time of the consultation and Survival Dependency some what disguised. Thus when both narcissistic parenting and double bind have been dealt with and there is still no shift, one must look for at least some aspect of Survival Dependency being present.

Life Limiting "Tools"

Frequently there is great guilt complicating the more superficial aspects of this dependency, but the basic problem will be the Belief that without dependency death will occur. Guilt, self-doubt, low self esteem are often "tools" used by the individual to keep himself dependent. Often the Entelechist will work with the individual to reverse self doubt, low self esteem, feelings of unworthiness, etc., only to find that what was believed to have been resolved still seems to be having a deleterious effect. The symptom has now simply become a "tool."

Originally, the individual took on the Belief that s/he must be unworthy, undeserving, etc. because of the patterns in his/her life. These beliefs also gave him/her the tools to demonstrate to a Protector/Rescuer/Caretaker that s/he needed to be taken care of. Thus, when the Entelechist helps the Survival Dependent to clear up the belief regarding such self-doubt, the Survival Dependent cannot let go of such thoughts and feelings because s/he needs them. S/he uses them to maintain his/her survival dependency and stay alive. Usually attempts to deal with such feelings and thoughts are ineffective until the belief in the need for dependency is dissolved. What seems to be "self sabotage" is actually a protective mechanism to survive.

Incubator Baby

An individual was in an incubator for over a month, the biological mother giving up the pre-mature baby for adoption.

When the adopting mother came in, the infant was so overjoyed at being loved and no longer alone, that it took on the Core Belief it must always have the mother around. This was the basis of the Survival Dependency she was experiencing as an adult.

Re-defining

The "swamp" for the Entelechist is: <u>anything</u> which seems to improve this individual is unconsciously seen as a threat to his/her survival! <u>Suggestions to better himself or herself in various ways are death threats</u>.

If the Entelechist continues to use such suggestions, the individual becomes uncomfortable during the session. At that point s/he may "fall asleep" or if hypnosis or some other altered state of consciousness is being used, come out of the trance state. During ordinary talk therapy, the individual may have difficulty following the Entelechist's statements and questions. It is like:

"My head has gone out to lunch!" It is common for such people to stop therapy if the Entelechist continues to use such "positive suggestions."

When the Entelechist has helped the individual through the Limiting Triad and the individual still does not report a sustained improvement in every area of his or her life, there almost always are Core Beliefs resulting in some form of Survival Dependency.

One of the simplest ways to access this information, even though the individual is denying it is true for him/her, is to simply ask the Non-Conscious Mind to create a symbol about his/her Core Beliefs in that arena.

Once uncovered, the individual has to be guided into "unfolding" out of the dependency rather than "improving" out of it, and this is best performed by the Non-Conscious portions of the mind.

Use of Hypnosis or Similar Altered States of Consciousness

We prefer to use the mental state achieved by asking the individual to set aside their Logical Mind and have it do no more than observe. Using their "Non-Conscious Mind" to allow pictures, thoughts, feelings and answers "pop" into mind. This process is describe in Chapters 13 & 14.

First, the individual's Logical Mind is asked to simply observe as the Non-Conscious Mind creates a symbol representing Survival Dependency. This process also asks the Non-Conscious Mind to correct or upgrade the symbol. The Logical Mind's job is to simply observe the changes that spontaneously occur – if any. No attempt is made to reason the individual out of the Core Belief.

Secondly, the individual with Survival Dependency is fearful of growing up regardless of how capable and mature they appear on the surface. This, too, is dealt with, usually as it arises in therapy, by encouraging the individual's Non-Conscious Mind to so deal with it.

Emphasis is placed on simply allowing the Non-Conscious Mind to do its job of problem solving, free of interference from the Logical Mind.

Chapter 14 explains all this in much more detail.

Signs of Recovery

Initial signs of becoming:

- happier
- healthier
- fewer problems in all areas
- current problems solved with effective solutions
- can tolerate being alone without becoming fearful
- becomes more successful
- does not use religious beliefs to limit improvement

Signs of Full Recovery:

Over a prolonged period of time:

- reports being happier for some time now
- reports certain physical symptoms or illness have disappeared
- reports fewer problems and that the solutions to problems do not cause more problems.

- can be alone or not in a relationship for some time and not fall apart.
- has love relationships which do not have evidence of pathological dependency.
- financial circumstances gradually improve and dependence on someone else for support ceases.

"Unfinished Business"

It is a natural need for children growing up in any circumstances to try to get the dominant parent to somehow acknowledge them. This can even happen in circumstances were the dominant parent is wonderful in every way, but somehow can not show the child physically and verbally that it is loved in the ways that every child needs. Consequently, the child goes to great lengths to some how "get blood out of a stone."

As previously mention, Louise was using her particular form of Survival Dependency to some how get expressions of love and caring from a father incapable of doing so. Thus, the "business" she had with him could never be resolved the way she wanted, no matter what she did or didn't do.

Chapter Ten covers "Unfinished Business" in much more detail.

As we will cover in the succeeding chapters, such attempts may continue on into adulthood distorting the child's, now an adult, life in every way.

Chapter Nine

The Personal Law of Survival

The child growing up in any or all aspects of the Triad and other factors mentioned in previous chapters, feels tremendously threatened. On some level, very simplistically, it knows it needs to have some way to insure its survival. At that point, the child either makes a decision to die or continue to live. If it chooses to die, then it will do so in some way. This may be by sudden illness, accidents, etc. If it chooses to live, then the child will structure a Personal Law of Survival. This Law will be uniquely designed according to the child's ability to reason out a modus operandi for survival *at that time and at the reasoning ability of its age level.*

This Personal Law of Survival is quite different than if had been structured by an adult. The individual putting together this basic rule of survival is young, immature, naïve, frightened, feeling helpless, angry and constantly defensive. It has no real knowledge of the ways of the world, what is really dangerous, and the most effective means to insure its survival. Because it is based on a desperate need to stay alive, it is maintained on through adulthood, unless something occurs to change the Core Belief we are calling "The Personal Law of Survival."

Intra-Uterine: If the child is yet to be born, still in the womb, it may "take on" that the way to survive is to duplicate the feelings it gets from the mother. According to such a personal law, after the child is born, it will repeatedly and cyclically experience whatever the mother was primarily feeling during the pregnancy.

If the mother was feeling sad, abandoned and guilty during the pregnancy, the unborn child absorbs those feelings and without any reasoning, "takes on" that "this is life."

From then on the child will consciously and unconsciously put itself into situations that generate such miserable feelings. If no such situation occurs, the child may find itself suddenly feeling such miserable feelings for no apparent reason. When this happens, the child, now an adult, may feel like s/he is having a nervous breakdown or going crazy. S/he is not going crazy, just simply repeating the feelings it has come to believe will insure its survival. A Personal Law of Survival taken on before birth.

The Need to Struggle As a Personal Law of Life

The Peri-natal experience (from conception to shortly after birth) may feel like one of repeated struggle to the child. Under such circumstances, the child may come into the outer physical world equating the feelings of struggle with the way life is to be once outside the womb. Such a child, now an adult, will have an life long history of consciously and unconsciously putting itself into circumstances and situations where the feelings of struggle are consistently present. In fact, they can not conceive of a world where such feelings are absent.

As previously mentioned in Chapter Nine, having a continuing pattern of struggle-producing problems is one way of doing this. Once you are aware of this possibility, it is usually quite easy to see if you have been caught up in such a pattern: For as far back as one can remember, there is always –always a problem of some kind that ranges from fairly major to near disaster that you have somehow overcome. It is characterized by struggling. There will always be something causing strong feelings of struggling. About the time one such problem has been solved, another is on your doorstep. Such problems causing you to struggle may cycle through various categories: health, family, financial, school, business, personal relationships, etc. – all filled with feelings of struggle.

The Need to be Under Pressure As a Personal Law of Life

While being under pressure may occur by having continuing struggles of one kind or another, the Core Belief in the need to be under pressure is quite separate from the Core Belief in struggle. As such, it must be specifically dealt with when it is present. Generally if you have this Core Belief, there is an ongoing sense of "being under pressure." It is a term you may frequently use describing yourself and your circumstances. You may find that before falling asleep some kind of worry or fear may come to mind each night. You may feel that you work best under pressure, and so you wait until the last minute to fulfill responsibilities. You may note that you often sit on the edge of your seat rather than relax back into it. Perhaps you may notice that your sitting posture is one that allows for rapidly standing up, even though there is no reason to do so.

People who believe in the need to struggle and/or be under pressure are often accused of being "drama queens" or "addicted to adrenalin." They may often put themselves in perilous situations

Callie

Callie came in to lose 15 lbs of excess weight that she could never seem to get rid of. If she lost it one month, it was back a few months later. If she gained more than the 15 lbs. she would easily lose every pound over that but not the 15 lbs. If she lost 20 lbs. she would rapidly gain 25 lbs. back. She had all three legs of the Triad and worked very well in dealing with these, except –the excess weight continued its usual pattern of fluctuation.

143

She reported priding herself on how well she worked with last minute deadlines. She often had sudden fears come up upon going to bed. She thought she smelled smoke. She heard somebody outside. She became concerned that she might be sabotaged by a co-worker. She had a history of TMJ (tempo-mandibular joint disease) She frequently discovered she was walking around with her teeth clenched. Often for no apparent reason. She suffered migraine headaches, during which she would ask people to hug her. What was frustrating, to both her and the Entelechist, was that there seemed to be no final resolution of her weight problem even though each of the key arenas involved were being resolved. She reported improvement in every other area of her life but her weight.

Reading an earlier version of this book, she suddenly found herself quite sleepy when she began to read the chapter on Survival Dependency. Over the next day she read the chapter in its entirety and realized that her survival dependency was between her and her mother. Her mother was seen as a "wolf" – and she was maintaining to protect herself from her mother and the world.

The next morning she awoke feeling a sense of relief. Something had shifted, so she was not quite so tense. Yet, still there was some presence of pressure.

While discussing this with the Entelechist, she spontaneously began to realize that what she had been calling "tension" was really "pressure." She noted that if she had nothing to do, she began to feel lifeless, "blah," sleepy, uninterested in anything and this might continue for several hours until suddenly her mind began to worry or recalled an unfinished project, and then she "came to life."

Working with her Non-Conscious Mind to develop and produce a symbol about her Core Beliefs regarding pressure, she had no picture, but a thought: "Pressure = life."

She had taken on, during the peri-natal period, that in order to feel alive, she had to feel pressure.

On occasion, the need to be under pressure in order to survive is powerfully connected with emotional expression. The very young child may become very fearful of expressing its feelings. This is usually related to an event which was interpreted by the child as requiring extremely limited or no emotional expression. In a sense, the child uses the pressure to "encase" its feelings so they are not released. Perhaps even to the extent that such feelings are not even recognized consciously but quickly repressed.

Bettie

"My father would do something if I showed any signs of joy or happiness, including laughing out loud. When I showed any of these feelings, he would do something that would take them away.

"My mother, however, would become very upset if I showed sadness, grief, anger, and similar emotions.

"So I quickly took on that I would have to not show any feelings at all. In a sense, I put myself under enough pressure all the time so I was not even aware that I was feeling any emotion!

"But if I became sick, if I had some sort of physical problem develop, I could show both the physical and the emotional feelings accompanying the physical illness! That my mother could accept and I certainly wasn't showing joy, happiness, pleasure etc. in such circumstances. Thus the interference of my father was also avoided. In other words, I took on the Core Belief that "being sick kept me safe."

"I attached to that the Belief that I could not 'do, be or have' what I wanted for fear of releasing taboo emotions."

The resulting life patterns Bettie developed: always some sort of physical illness that never became too bad or a lot better. Never getting what she wanted. Focusing on a "past life" that the cause of taking on the Belief about not "do, be or have" was due to being blamed for seducing a priest and tortured for it. She was terrified of becoming an adult, even though she was far into chronological adulthood. She had been on welfare for years, becoming sick in some way if she began to be able to financially take care of herself.

As the reader may have noted by now, it is extremely important to allow feelings to move through your body and be fully and completely expressed. Cultural mores may seem to forbid such expression as in: "big boys don't cry." However, it is the familial teachings in the first 6 years or so that are the most powerful controllers.

The Need To Struggle—The Need To Be Under Pressure

Such individuals will usually report that:

1. They cannot relax, or at least, not for more than a very short time.
2. They always need to be doing something mentally and/or physically.
3. They tend to do a lot of worrying or fretting, especially when they first go to bed or when they get quiet.
4. There is always some kind of problem going on.
5. They may have a sense of humor, but are never really happy for long.
6. They may have difficulty completing things.
7. They may have difficulty living in one place for long.
8. They may have difficulty managing money, especially windfalls.
9. They tend to sit as though they might have to suddenly get up.
10. They may have problems comfortably relating to others around them.
11. They may find themselves as members of groups that are short lived.

12. They may have a pattern of not allowing themselves to get what they want or, if they do, they don't allow themselves to keep it.
13. They may be "high strung" and easily irritated.
14. They may report a birth that was prolonged or difficult in some way, and perhaps, requiring forceps delivery.
15. They may report the obstetrician recommending a trial of labor to see if their head could pass on down, but such progress was blocked and, after awhile, a cesarean section was done.
16. They may report being held back during the delivery for whatever reason.
17. They may go through life with a sense of having to be "on guard" all or most of the time,
18. They may report that they "always seem to have something wrong with me."
19. They may report that they feel unworthy or undeserving to have/keep what they want.
20. They may report that somehow they will die if life is easy or they have no problems.
21. They may feel that this is a way to feel alive.
22. They may be accused of being "drama queens" or "adrenalin junkies."
23. At first they may have enjoyed and taken pride in solving their problems and those of other people, but are now tired of doing so – but somehow can't quit.
24. They may be accident prone.
25. They may report feeling it is dangerous to settle in one place or not be on the move,
26. They may be a perfectionist,
27. They may become easily discouraged and make only half hearted efforts,
28. They may have difficulty completing things, often because of the fear that something bad will happen if they successfully complete.
29. They may be chronically late.

30. They may have minor illnesses that "hang on."
31. They may put off things to the last minute.
32. They feel they only get their work done, or work best. when under pressure.
33. They often set themselves up so they have too much to do in too short a time.
34. They often go through repeated restricted or strange diets.
35. They may do very well when they are struggling or putting themselves under pressure, because this is what they were taught to do while growing up.

The Belief in the need to struggle and/or be under pressure is usually powerfully connected to survival. While one may lead to the other, each must be worked with separately.

The Triad

The Personal Law of Survival taken on in circumstances we call the "Triad," result in the symptoms previously described in preceding chapters. Often such symptoms are an expression or the result of the Personal Law of Survival.

Sudden Traumatic Emotional Reversal

The most commonly encountered Personal Law of Survival encountered here is the use of the Defcon warning system. Using the miserable feelings of the original event, in degrees, to protect the child from ever experiencing such a threat to life again.

Re-Defining the Personal Law of Survival

There are three approaches.

1. Accessing the Core Belief that is the Personal Law of Survival and logically re-structuring it.
2. Accessing the Core Belief that is the Personal Law of Survival in the form of a symbol created by the Non-Conscious Mind and using the Logical Mind to modify the symbol appropriately.
3. Accessing the Core Belief that is the Personal Law of Survival away from the awareness of the Logical Mind in whatever way the Non-Conscious Mind chooses to do so. Remind the individual that "things are different now," and "you never learn less." Leaving the correction completely up to the Non-Conscious Mind's corrective process.

In the authors' experience, the first approach can be used with Core Beliefs taken on around the age of 7 or later. Unfortunately, the Personal Law of Survival is usually well in place by the age of 6. If it was modified after age 7 or 8, the modification may be corrected logically, but usually the basic Law will not change much. Too, when you use logic to solve a problem, various fears, guilts and limitations automatically come up and interfere with a truly valid solution.[44]

The second approach is the one we used for many years. The symbolic approach is a much more comfortable means of examining some very uncomfortable material. The Non-Conscious Mind is asked to create a symbol representing the problem. The Logical Mind is then asked to evaluate it and change the symbol to something more appropriate.

---

[44] See Chapter 13.

However, it too, is subjected to the same problems with the Logical Mind as in the first approach.

The third approach currently seems to be the most effective as well as the gentlest. Basically, the individual is asked to keep his or her Logical Mind simply as an observer and to take no part in making any decisions or evaluations while hearing certain suggestions. The Logical Mind functions here as a "reporter" not a "commentator." The individual is reminded that every thing s/he hears is being directed at the Non-Conscious Mind only.

The Non-Conscious Mind is the problem solver and as previously discussed during the consultation, has much more information available to it than the Logical Mind. The Logical Mind's functions are to evaluate and set goals.

The Non-Conscious Mind's functions include creating the symbols, answering any questions and solving the problems.[45]

---

[45] Chapter 13

Chapter Ten

"Unfinished Business"

Every child wants and needs physical and verbal expressions of being loved, cared about, and approved of, as s/he grows up. This is a natural part of development and strengthens the child in many ways.

Also, on some level, the child realizes that his or her survival depends on the attitudes of the dominant parent, and spends much of his or her developing years seeking those messages that somehow this child is okay with this parent. While many children go through childhood frequently receiving such messages, there are those who would have been satisfied to experience it just once as long as it was clear and heartfelt!

Unfortunately, this kind of parent, has his or her own Core Beliefs that prevent such a response. So no matter what the parental figure really feels and thinks about the child and no matter what the child does, the desired responses cannot occur. Since the child realizes that a parent is supposed to love the child, the child mistakenly assumes that s/he is at fault in someway, or that kind of treatment is "love." The need is still there and active, and so the older child, moving into the teenage years and beyond, unconsciously seeks another person who will symbolically be that parent. This other person, this symbolic parent, is then expected to give this young adult what the "real" parent could not. This is doomed to failure, because the symbolic parent must be like the real parent in at least one key way: emotionally unavailable!

And so the child, now an adult, moves through various relationships throughout its adult years "falling in love" with emotionally unavailable people because the child, now an adult, is unconsciously seeking to complete what they wanted from the real parental figure. This is what we mean by "Unfinished business."

To find out for yourself, create a comparison list:

Mother and Spouse or Lover

All the ways in which they are similar All the ways in which they are different

1.	1.
2.	2.
3.	3. etc.
4.	
5. etc.	

Father and Spouse or Lover

All the similarities All the ways they are different

1.	1.
2.	2. etc.
3.	
4.	
5. etc.	

Make a list of all the similarities and then ask yourself, "Why marry or have a love relationship with someone who has all these similarities to my parents?"

In very rare instances, there will be no similarities, in which case, ask yourself, "why marry or have a love relationship with someone so different from my parents?"

This can also be done with each person you have become emotionally involved in.

It can also be done with problem individuals with whom you work.

The Solution

The solution to Unfinished Business is the realization, that if you couldn't get the kind of acknowledgement and love you wanted from your dominant parent, how are you ever going to get it from someone like them? You can't get blood out of a stone, even if the stone wished it could give it to you. How they treated you had nothing to do with proving whether or not you are of value, loveable, acceptable, etc.

It becomes important to accept your parents for who and what they were. Let go of that life long drive to change them and their responses to you. It is not your problem or fault that they are that way. It is their own Core Beliefs.

And then, to get the kind of acknowledgement and love you want, pick someone who is quite capable of doing so.

Chapter Eleven

Forgiveness

The reader should be aware that the processes of forgiveness described near the end of this chapter are very powerful and effective. Reading <u>and putting into practice</u> the material in books such as "Forgiveness: The Greatest Healer of All"[46] is also of great benefit. However, because of our tendency to block unpleasant things from our awareness, the reader may need professional help in accessing and forgiving what needs to be forgiven.

Letting Go

Forgiveness has been defined as "letting go."

It is important for any one suffering from any aspect of the Triad to eventually forgive. It is especially necessary for those suffering from Lizzie Borden Rage to reach a comfortable state of forgiveness regarding individuals and events in their past. A "comfortable" state is one that is truly neutral. "Truly neutral" means that such memories are about as emotionally upsetting as the average person experiences tying their shoes.

This is why it is of value to consider that "a memory is a memory is a memory."

Each memory exists for us with various beliefs and labels attached to it. Particularly "reference memories" that are those memories we use to prove our beliefs.

---

[46] *Forgiveness: The Greatest Healer of All*, G. Jampolsky, Beyond Words Publishers, Hillsboro, Oregon, 1999

And of course, no memory is 100% accurate where youth and/or trauma is involved.

A Memory, Is a Memory, Is a Memory

What is the difference between the memory of an event in a dream and the memory of a childhood event "in real life," or any memory - even one concerning what happened a few minutes ago?

Only the beliefs and the labels attached to the memory.

Otherwise there is no difference.

It is commonly known that anything you intensely imagine will be accepted by your mind as having actually happened. This is often encountered where you may vividly rehearses what you are going to say to another person and then find you have a "memory" of already having done so. The other person is unaware of this, and is surprised when you acts as though the discussion has already taken place.

"Reference Memories" are those memories we used to prove our Core Beliefs are true. Since the younger one is when storing such a memory, the more distorted the memory. The more upset one is when storing such a memory, the more distorted the memory.

We tend to live our lives based on beliefs that are based on a distorted past. To compound the felony, we use that reference memory to predict our future and how to handle it. Truly, in such instances: The Past Is Prologue To The Future!

Do you carry eternal hatred for someone because of what they did to you in a dream? Probably not. This is because you have defined the dream memory as "unreal." You might be emotionally upset for an hour or so on awakening, but you know it wasn't "real" and it soon fades away.

Do you carry eternal hatred for someone because of what they did to you in a memory of an event at age 6? Could be, because you define this one as "real." And you may carry the mental, emotional and physical upset forever.

But in both cases, your functioning is based on your definition of which was real and which was not.

Skillful questioning by someone else may result in you having a great deal of difficulty coming up with hard evidence to prove the memory at age 6 really happened.

You might say: "Well, I have this scar to prove it!" Okay, so you have a scar but all you really have is a memory that you believe explains its presence and "therefore proves it."

You might say: "My sister gave me that scar when we fought over a bicycle."

Your sister might say: "You got that scar when you fell down riding your bicycle."

Both of you believe your memory of the scar to be accurate.

They are similar, but they are not the same – although the two of you may "negotiate" an agreement about it with further discussion. However, that does not prove that negotiation of the scar's meaning is true either.

All this is simply groundwork to help you move into a state of forgiveness.

Being unforgiving of yourself and/or others only causes you great harm. The other person may be dead, or totally oblivious to what you remember they did or didn't do to you.

You are the only one still suffering – day after day.

Consider what it means to forgive—to be forgiving:

FORGIVE: The basic roots of the word means, "to give away, to give up resentment against, to give up the desire to punish, to stop being angry with, to pardon, to give up all claim to punish or exact penalty for an offense, to overlook, to cancel or remit, as a debt, fine or penalty, to pardon, absolve, remit, cancel, release."

Perhaps as you allow yourself to consider these meanings of the word: "forgive," you might also consider the price one pays for being unforgiving, for not letting go.

Being Unforgiving Is Expensive

The person who is unforgiving actually feels angry, defensive and helpless.

Got that?

If you are feeling unforgiving about something, it is almost certain that accompanying that rigidity are feelings of being angry, defensive and helpless. This rigidity is causing you great physical and emotional harm.

You might have to look a little deeper for your helpless feelings to come into your awareness, as that is a very scary feeling. It is only those who believe they are unable to do anything otherwise, that become unforgiving.

Stubbornness may feel like power, but it actually is an expression of feeling helpless.

They may believe that by not forgiving they protect themselves from further damage or harm. Instead, being unforgiving causes them great damage and harm.

They may believe they are getting even or achieving revenge by being unforgiving. They are not!

Who or what they do not forgive is not really damaged in any way.

When you exercise your autonomy, your power, your control by choosing not to forgive, you are unconsciously reminding yourself that you are weak and helpless in the light of what happened.

As long as you choose not to forgive, you are consciously and un-consciously reminding yourself of such helplessness and weakness every time you consciously or unconsciously think of that person.

Such feelings of helplessness and weakness can spill over into other aspects of your life by causing you to restrict yourself with fear and doubt in a wide variety of areas.

Fear of Forgiving

Perhaps you believe that if you do not forgive that person it will damage or harm them in some way. and perhaps it does for the moment—particularly if they love you and wish to make amends.

For the most part though, the people you do not forgive are often totally unaware of your grievance or grudge towards them. They have no conscious memory of the event (or at least not the same memory) which you have chosen to refuse to forgive, regardless of how much pain and anxiety you think you are causing them, by not forgiving them.

The real recipient of the pain and anxiety is you. You are the one who remains miserable – limited and restricted. Tied up in chains of your own making, held in place by your own thinking. When you choose not to forgive, you are telling yourself that you are weak and helpless. That the only way you can feel that you have any control over the situation is to internalize the pain and anger you are feeling.

If you were coming from strength and confidence you would use that strength and confidence to resolve the grudge or grievance completely so it had no effect upon you, *regardless of the other person's reactions.*

Perhaps you believe that the only effect it has on you is to somehow give you a sense of autonomy, power or control over the circumstances or person. In truth, if you really felt powerful and in control, you would forgive. You would rush to forgive and let go completely. It is only in the areas we feel weak and helpless that we may become unforgiving.

Weakness and helplessness generate anger, tension, pain and depression within your body.

Forgiveness brings out your strength, confidence and eliminates the above mentioned life limiting feelings. When you stay unforgiving you choose to keep the life limiting feelings. You hold them within. You may consciously or unconsciously even select in which body part or organ you are going to carry the anger, the tension, the pain, the weakness, the helplessness.

We call this "the Organ of Expression."[47]

You have shifted into using physical symptoms of a particular part of your body to express certain emotions. And so that body part becomes diseased ("dis-eased.").

Can Being Unforgiving Cause Disease?

Perhaps you believe it is important to keep your grievance or grudge, and yet at the same time you wish to be mentally and physically healed. How can you heal a mind, or a part of your body, if it seems more important to keep the grudge or grievance when, at the same time, you are putting all the anger, pain, tension, weakness and helplessness you feel about it into that body part? Perhaps it has become more important to you to keep the miserable feelings and so keep them in that particular body part. This body part may eventually become truly organically diseased. Simply maintaining a "tension" in that body part affects the vascular, lymphatic and cellular functioning. Try playing the piano with your hand clenched into a fist. So you are still unforgiving and you have the added problem of certain physical symptoms. Such physical symptoms are

---

[47] *Belief, Emotions and Disease*, J. and C. Spear (privately published)

often quite difficult to permanently rid oneself of – that is, until forgiveness occurs.

One of the authors (CAS) worked with a highly intelligent woman who had chronic bronchitis. It was complicated by an antibiotic-resistant pseudomonas secondary infection. For many months her physicians had tried a variety of treatments and medications to clear it up.

The bronchitis and the secondary infection disappeared when this lady strongly voiced her rage at her husband.

She was enraged that all he wanted to be was a carpenter.

She thought that like she and her adult children, he should hold some position of great importance. Once she fully expressed the anger and realize the grudge she held against him, she was willing to let him be the way he wanted to be.

If maintaining our grudges and grievances does little, if any damage to those we chose not to forgive and instead does great continuous damage to ourselves; is it worth the price you are paying?

Is it truly all right for you to be healthier?

It is truly all right for you to be happier if the only thing blocking your road to health and happiness is the grudges and grievances you are holding within? Would you rather be happy or "right?"

Is it not worth eliminating that block from your life, your mind and your body? If only to find out for sure?

When you choose to come from strength and confidence instead of weakness, helpless, anger, pain and tension; when you choose to use your autonomy, your power, your control to correct the situation *within you* (and it is within you), it no longer continues to create helplessness, weakness, tension, pain and anger throughout you. Your mind and various parts of your body work more healthfully and more naturally. Certain disease processes within you may disappear entirely. If that is all right with you.

Forgiveness and Healing

The healing of our emotions and our body requires two things:

1. Forgiving the grudges and grievances we are carrying around within us.
2. The willingness to give up the symptoms of the disease

Perhaps it is time to consider the actual price you have been paying by carrying around your grudges and your grievances. Somebody once said: "The best revenge is living well." By "living well" we mean that you have come to allow yourself to activate increasingly more of your potential and live a life that is happy, successful, loving and healthy. You have learned that this increasingly results with your willingness to forgive – to let it go completely. You are fulfilling your entelechy.

Forgetting What or Whom to Forgive

Perhaps you have directly or indirectly chosen to keep the mental and physical damage by staying unwilling to forgive. Perhaps you think you have forgotten who you need to forgive in order to release yourself from certain emotional or physical symptoms. Perhaps you think you have forgotten what happened to cause you to take on the grudge or grievance. Perhaps you think that what that person did to you is so monstrous it can never be forgiven.

The important thing is to become at least neutral about the whole thing within your mind. By being "neutral," we mean that recall of the event has no more effect on you than any other unimportant action of the day.

It was something that happened and you have exercised your autonomy, your power, your control to forgive it. You have let go of it. You can truly say to that person or group: "I wish you well," and mean it. Recalling the event or events truly generates no emotion in you.

Perhaps it is like walking from one room to another.

Walking through the doorway generates no emotion. You are simply leaving one area and moving into another. Moving from a cold, freezing room into a comfortable, warm room generates a feeling of relief as you move from the cold to the comfortable, and the memory of the cold room and its discomfort is left behind automatically.

It is no longer important. At some point you even forget that you were in that cold room. That does not mean that you would spend a lot of time in a cold room again.

Physical Symptoms

If you have various physical symptoms, it is important to realize and understand that you may be holding some sort of grievance or grudge against this person or persons, that in turn has been causing your mind to distort your body. I am quite sure that whatever this person did or failed to do was very important at that time. Perhaps you felt attacked, betrayed, abandoned, whatever. That in some way, this person somehow "sinned" against you or you against them; and so this emotional or physical symptom or disease seemed to become necessary. Consider now if you had a dream when you were sleeping last night and in this dream this person acted in such a way. You would give it no credence. You would attach no importance to it. You might even laugh about it when talking to that person the next morning. Of course you would hold no grudge or grievance because it was only a dream. Nothing real happens in a dream because you control the dream. It is your mind that develops the symbols and events within the dream.

After all – it is only a dream.

After all – it is only the memory of a dream.

Consider now that it has been suggested that the life you lead when you are not asleep is not the real reality. That it too, is a dream each of us creates for ourselves. Giving ourselves a particular ego or personality; seeing each person in our world as a particular ego or personality. Consider this person who somehow wronged you—wronged you in your memory of a waking dream we call "physical reality." What then is the importance of his, her, or their actions?

A character in a dream can do you no harm; can do you no wrong, unless you carry a grudge or grievance because of it all. What would it be like to carry a grudge because of your memory of what a character in a dream "did" to you? No difference. Then it doesn't make any difference, because what does make the difference – to you – is the beliefs and attitudes you attach to the memory. The way you hold it in your mind. The way you have it stored in memory.

Perhaps you have been looking for a way to heal. Perhaps you have been wondering what it takes to release yourself from this emotional or physical symptom or disease.

It takes forgiveness and a decision. A decision that it is more important to you to be free of this physical symptom or disease and to help achieve that by forgiving. Truly forgiving so you are internally at peace about it as well.

Among the healthiest, happiest people are those who have learned to forgive and let go of anger, resentment, desire for revenge and all the other aspects that unforgiving people distort their minds and their bodies with.

Fear of Forgiving

Some people fear to forgive. They believe that if they forgive it would mean they might allow someone to "do that to me again" or that the perpetrator would not be punished. He or she would not have learned their lesson. He or she would have gotten away with something, got away "Scott free." Or, that the person who forgives somehow loses his or her power and control, or that the person who forgives would some how lose his or her motivation to stay alive, be successful, whatever.

Some people believe that as long as they do not forgive, that will some how keep them alive. Their belief is that the so-called negative feelings associated with being unforgiving – hate, anger, rage, revenge and so on, some how enables the unforgiving individual to stay alive simply by continuing to feel such miserable feelings.

Fortunately or unfortunately, continuing to be unforgiving about anything or even one thing or person costs the unforgiving individual an enormous amount of pain, loss, discomfort, failure and other undesirable circumstances, simply because they refuse to let it go. They have come to believe that somehow this has an effect on the person they refuse to forgive, but which actually has its greatest devastating effects on themselves. The person who fails to forgive pays an enormous price in the physiological devastation in his or her body. Its various parts are subjected to this devastation almost minute by minute of each day. Many so-called psycho-somatic disorders are unconsciously maintained by being unforgiving of some one or some thing.

Zorina

Zorina had come to the United States when she was about 30 years old. She worked for her sponsor and eventually was making a good living and fell in love. He was a handsome man and very attentive. Her best friend kept telling her what a wonderful man she had. She trusted this man in every way. One day she returned home early and found him and her best friend very busy making love.

She went into a rage, striking out at both of them with whatever she could find as they fled the house.

She came to us some years later complaining of depression.

She also had mild high blood pressure and indigestion. It was quickly revealed that she still harbored that rage against friend and lover. She could not, she would not forgive them even though she knew it was only harming her. Any quiet moment was filled with the recall of that horrible moment. She would not date again. She would not allow anyone close to her. In a sense, she loved the hate and anger she continually carried within her.

At one point during her therapy, she reported that she was to have tests to find out where her indigestion was coming from. They had told her (this was before MRI's and CAT scans) that they thought she might have gall stones along with some liver dysfunction. We talked about her feelings towards friend and lover and how it was destroying her life. It was casually mentioned that with the surgery, perhaps she might "cut out" those feelings.

She came back after the surgery to report that they had found an inoperable cancer in her liver. She said she was well aware that her feelings towards friend and lover somehow caused the cancer, but it was just as well as she really did not want to live. As with Zorina, the unforgiving cannot process daily events and experiences as they are but instead sees them through the distortion of being unforgiving. Consequently:

165

- They usually carry a feeling that something is wrong or missing.
- They usually blame others, not realizing that when they blame they give away their power.
- They feel they cannot allow themselves to be who and what they truly are.
- The most expensive price paid by the unforgiving is that they develop progressive conscious loss of who and what they really are, and of the wonderful feelings of life that is part of the essence of who and what they are.
- They must be unreal.

The unforgiving person cannot be unforgiving and at the same time carry the conscious awareness of their very essence and its wondrous feelings. In other words, to feel happy, successful, loving and similar expansive feelings are denied them by the mechanics of what they use to avoid being forgiving.

They cannot let go.

If they cannot let go, they must tighten up.

They tighten up in all the various dimensions of their body, mind and spirit.

So they gradually, or rapidly, consciously deny themselves in order to stay unforgiving.

What a terrible price to pay for something that only exists now within your mind within your memory banks.

By simply, and steadily, completely forgiving each person, each event, each circumstance that requires forgiving, you would automatically allow your body to restore itself to a healthier state.

You restore or acquire a deep sense of peace, joy and satisfaction along with powerful feelings of autonomy, acceptance, belonging, safety and security, self worth, self esteem and your connection to Who or What you pray to.

Of course, you may stay unforgiving.

Of course, you may continue to seek revenge.

Of course, you may continue to hate and resent and whatever else accompanies your special interests in being unforgiving.

Of course, you may use that to prove you are right and they are wrong. Asking yourself: "Would I rather be right than happy?"

Two questions for the unforgiving person to ask himself or herself:

1. Would I rather be right or happy...?
2. Am I completely innocent? Have I never done anything to anyone or anything that I should have sought forgiveness?

It is very important to understand that forgiveness is never for the benefit of the other person.

It is always for your benefit.

When you forgive and let go, you release your potential.

You release increasingly more of your entelechy

Forgiving Yourself

Among the most difficult things to do, especially for the young, naïve, developing child, is to be forgiving of oneself. At various times, between the onset of your being and your present age, you may have taken on some guilt about:

who you are,
what you did or didn't do,
what you should have done,
what you almost did,
what you should not have done,

and at that time, or soon afterwards, came to believe that such thoughts, such acts, were unforgivable and you were to be punished, limited, contained, and/or restricted forever. Because that was somehow supposed to make you a better person or prevent you from being a bad or worse person. Perhaps at various times between the onset of your being and your present age you may have taken on, from others around you, that you were horribly guilty:

> if you didn't do what they wanted,
> if you did what you wanted to,
> if you didn't feel what they wanted you to feel,
> if you felt what you wanted to feel,
> you had done something unforgivable.

Thus, you were unforgivable, bad, dangerous and needed to be punished, limited, contained and restricted **"forever."** Perhaps at various times between the onset of your being and your present age, you may have taken on from various religious figures, various religions, evangelists, missionaries, and other church or church-like authorities that you were guilty of unforgivable sin, perhaps even evil, and were to be punished, limited, contained, restricted **"forever."**

Perhaps the same happened to you in schools, jobs, peer groups, siblings—whomever—wherever—whenever. It makes no difference when, where or who it was, for now both the accuser and the victim in all this is yourself. If you are feeling guilty, then you do what you can do to correct the results of your actions. At that point, the guilt feelings should cease and you go on with your life, free of guilt. Even when you have done the unforgivable, the correct solution is to see what you did, or failed to do, that was wrong, correct it (if possible), make a mental note to never let it happen again and forgive yourself…and go on.

In other words, forgive yourself and go on with your life. The long term effects of feeling guilty results in you gradually suppressing your abilities and talents. This results in *denying those gifts to yourself, the people you care about and the world. With that denial, you are the one who suffers the most.* Perhaps you have a pretty clear idea as to who would be better off, besides yourself, if you were free of guilt feelings and had completely forgiven yourself. Thus, be free to activate much more of your potential and realize much more of your entelechy. Perhaps you have a vague idea as to who would be better off, besides yourself, if you were free of guilt feelings and had completely forgiven yourself.

The secret to all this is simply the recognition that regardless of whatever and whenever and from whomever you took on that you had committed the unforgivable, *you are not the same person now that you were the*n.

The punishments, rules, limitations; the restrictions no longer apply, regardless of what you have consciously and unconsciously been feeling guilty about – and unforgiving of yourself.

The problem is, that if left up to your Logical Mind there are those so-called "unforgivable acts" that you would completely overlook and there are others you could not even consciously remember even though they are still affecting you. And in most instances, those unforgivable acts of childhood would be seen as of no importance, or even ridiculous, if observed while you were an adult.

Chapter Twelve

Using Dreams

Informative Dreams

Informative dreams are those dreams, that for our purposes here, occur in order to access and reveal deeply held information about what is troubling you. We will also discuss ways of using such dreams to correct what is troubling you.

Intuition (Hunches)

Some years ago, two groups of businessmen were interviewed. One group were men who had gone bankrupt and the other group were highly successful in their businesses. Each one was asked how he made business decisions. Everyone said they gathered all the facts, learning as much as they could about business management, their product, what the competition was doing, the best rates of financing, etc. There was one difference between the two groups. The group that went bankrupt said that if they had a hunch or a feeling that the logical answer was wrong, they would still follow the logical answer and ignore the hunch. The group that was highly successful said that if they had a hunch or a feeling that the logical answer was wrong, they would not follow the logical answer and instead would go with the hunch.

When purely logical reasoning is followed and the "nudgings" from our Non-Conscious Minds are ignored, the correct answer or response is often obliterated from our choices. Over and over again you will hear people from all walks of life, in all kinds of circumstances, say: "I had a feeling that I shouldn't do that and I did." "I had a feeling that I should go another way, but I ignored it and got into trouble."

The "scientific method" has no place for such input and so there is a huge source of knowledge that it is ignoring or, at worst, calling "superstition" or "nonsense."

Dreams

The everyday man in the street is quite aware of dreams and that they have meanings of various kinds and can be of value.

There are still scientists who believe they are simply neuro-chemical firings in the brain that really have no meanings. There were also people who continued to believe the earth was flat (a society in England), until finally they were convinced the pictures from space were not faked.

Reminding yourself before sleep to have an informative dream, is a highly effective way to use your dreams to get information about your self, emotional problems, or any other kind of problems.

Dreaming The Way Out Of A Mental Institution

Many years ago, Milton Erickson, M. D. described a process for using dreams that he developed to work with patient in a mental institution. The particular patient was not responding to other psychiatrists and Erickson, a psychiatric resident at the time, was assigned the case.

He eventually was able to help the patient enter a hypnotic state. He then suggested to the patient that he would have an informative dream that night as to why he was having the emotional problems that landed him in the hospital.

The next day the dream was reported to him and Erickson again asked him to go into hypnosis. Using the hypnotic state, Erickson then suggested that he would have the same dream again, only with a different cast of characters, a little nearer, a little clearer and with a little more understanding.

This process was repeated daily. Over a period of time, the patient began to recall his dreams and to understand his real problem.

This treatment resulted in a successful conclusion and the patient was discharged from the hospital.

Fortunately, it is not necessary for one to receive these suggestions in hypnosis in order to do something similar.

Using Informative Dreams

An individual with a physical, psychological or any kind of problem can begin by suggesting to himself the first night: I want to have an informative dream about my _____." When you wake up, either during the night or in the morning, or whenever you remember the dream, record it on tape or write it down.

Example 1: You have a chronic rash that you have tried for years to get rid of. Using Informative Dreaming you would start the first night by suggesting *just before you fall asleep* "I want to have an informative dream about my rash."

Example 2: Who or what is it I need to forgive and why? FIRST NIGHT: Write out on a piece of paper the *Immediate Pre-Sominal Direction* ©: [48]

---

[48] Note: Immediate Pre-sominal Direction is that direction given to yourself just before you turn out the lights and roll over to go to sleep. Pre-sominal means "before sleep." Delayed Pre-sominal Direction is one given over 30 minutes before going to sleep.

"I WANT TO HAVE AN INFORMATIVE DREAM ABOUT_____.

Write down whatever you remember of the dream when you awaken. Briefly note the key points of the dream here.

SECOND NIGHT:

"I want to have the same informative dream again about _____ only a little nearer, a little clearer and with a different cast of characters." Key points of the dream:

THIRD NIGHT:

"I want to have the same informative dream again about _____ only a little nearer, a little clearer, with more understanding and with a different cast of characters." Key points of the dream:

FOURTH NIGHT:

"I want to have the same informative dream again about _____ only a little nearer, a little clearer, with more understanding and with a different cast of characters." Key points of the dream:

FIFTH NIGHT:

"I want to have the same informative dream again about _____ only a little nearer, a little clearer, with more understanding and a different cast of characters." Key points of the dream:

SIXTH NIGHT:

"I want to have the same informative dream again about _____ only a little nearer, a little clearer, with more understanding and a different cast of characters." Key points of the dream:

SEVENTH NIGHT:

"I want to have the same informative dream again about _____ only a little nearer, a little clearer, with more understanding and a different cast of characters." Key points of the dream: Usually you will begin to see as pattern or perhaps have a flash of insight as to what is really going on. SUMMARY OF DREAM PATTERN THIS WEEK IF ANY RECALLED:

By following such a process, you may discover very clear messages as to what is the cause of your "dis-ease."

Therapeutic Use of Informative Dreams

These same dreams may be used therapeutically to help you resolve your problem, without ever having to try to interpret your dreams.

When you remember the dream, run the pictures through your mind again and change the ending so it *feels right*. It doesn't make any difference whether you remember the dream on awakening, in the middle of the night or standing in the shower two days later.

By changing the ending so it *feels right*, you are taking the symbols created by your non-conscious mind and using them to change the Core Beliefs they represent.

Your Core Beliefs structure the dream symbols. As you change those symbols and the way they interact, you are modifying your Core Beliefs in that area, at the same time. This might be called "reverse engineering."

What do we mean by "feels right." It means a change in the dream ending that feels comfortable to you. One that does not give you any sense of anxiety. An ending that feels right, may not seem to be right logically. When confronted by such a choice, an ending that feels right or an ending that does not feel right, but is logically correct, use the ending that feels right. Do not use the logical one.

Sometimes dreams are very symbolic such as dreaming of orange triangles. You see the orange triangles in your mind's eye again and experiment with changing the shapes and colors. Finally it *feels right* to make them circles and keep the orange color. You have no idea why, it just feels right. That is what you do. Remember it is what "feels right," not what "feels good," although the two may go along together.

Sometimes a dream may seem to be simply a replay of something that happened recently, like a memory. Nevertheless, you consider everything and everyone in the dream as symbols, and change the ending so it feels right. It does not make any difference what the real people or the real event was. It is the images of the dream that we are working with and upgrading. This is usually the most comfortable and effective ways to use dreams to effect a major shift in your life. It does so at a rate that is in line with the shifting and upgrading of your Core Beliefs.

Therapeutic Dreaming

If you are really ready, there is a very rapid way to make such a shift: Transformative Dreaming. Be aware, that if you try Transformative Dreaming before you are really ready, it may bring up whatever is blocking your improvement. It usually does this by having it occur in your day to day life.

Example:
If you ask for a Transformative Dream releasing you to make more money in your life while your Core Belief about such success is that it is dangerous to your safety, you may

find yourself having to deal with the old safety issues you have had connected to money in the past.

An Alternative Method [49]

Upon being in bed and ready to go to sleep, give yourself the following suggestions:

"I want to have a problem solving dream during this sleep period…a dream that solves a very important problem for me…(state the problem)…a dream that solves this very important problem for me…by giving me the answers to 3 questions and then putting the solution into action:

1. What is the problem?
2. What caused it?
3. How can I get rid of it safely and harmlessly?

…I will have such a dream, remember it and understand it…upon awaking I will vividly recall this dream…record it and become aware of its meaning about what the problem is…and the solution to my problem as I do so."…(You may find it of value to record this on a audio cassette and listen to it as you fall asleep.) and then after having that problem solving dream…returning to sleep…either in that sleep period or the next one…and having your Non-Conscious Mind put into action that solution if it hasn't already done so…

Be sure to write down or record any fragment of a dream that you remember, even if it does not seem to be related to the problem you are working with.

As example #2 demonstrates, such dreams may be directed more specifically, for example: "forgiveness dreams."

---

[49] Note: This is [roughly] based on a Silva Mind Control Technique

Using one or both of the above approaches requesting problem solving dreams will result in dream symbols that somehow represents:

1. What needs to be forgiven, and
2. direction and guidance into truly forgiving them/you for whatever it was, as represented by the dreams and, then,
3. bringing such forgiveness for every single aspect up into your outer day to day world, and perhaps
4. giving you an even deeper understanding that will enable you to forgive all the others you need to forgive, and so unfold into completely forgiving yourself and your world safely, harmlessly, easily, effortlessly and appropriately. So that you are free to be all that you were meant to be. Releasing all your potential and moving you into being the highest and finest you are capable of being: your entelechy

Chapter Thirteen

Therapeutic Considerations

In the first twelve chapters we have given you some tools and information to better understand yourself. Hopefully you realize at this point, that if you have one or more of the problems previously described you are not crazy or insane.

You have been simply following Core Belief decisions made when you were very naïve and young. Moving out of all this is basically a matter of changing your mind. Changing deeply held Core Beliefs based on a child's reasoning. A true self-help book would give you a step by step process to free you from whatever limiting Core Beliefs you are functioning under.

If the section on Dreams and on Forgiveness has not helped you to accomplish that, remember that limiting Core Beliefs are just that: limiting. Don't be surprised if you haven't accomplished freedom from such limiting. If we believe we need to be limited to survive, get love, etc. then until those Core Beliefs are changed, not much improves for very long. What happens when an individual has at least one of the limiting triad and various other approaches fail to correct the thinking?

The authors have found that in dealing with their own limiting Core Beliefs, a trusted outside source is required to help you "see the forest for the trees."

Behavior modification, cognitive therapy, hypnotherapy and other approaches in skilled hands may work very well for you. The authors have found with some individuals, that the usual logical (cognitive) approaches rarely work. Particularly if there is more than one "leg" of the triad –

especially if there is material stemming from the peri-natal period.

In other words, the usual "talk therapy" is often only temporarily effective. At some point the individual begins to feel "stuck" and repeats the life limiting cycle over and over again. Great strides may be made in therapy, various traumatic events elicited and re-structured. It may seem as though every thing has been taken care of.

However, a few days or weeks, or even a year later, it seems as thought it has all returned.

Consequently, the authors utilize the PreP process described in Chapter 13.

Order of Therapeutic Approach

In utilizing such a process, we have found that the order in which each limiting aspect is approached and worked with is extremely important. This is because with more than one "leg" active, improvements in that aspect may be held in abeyance by one of the other "legs." Too, coupled with this may be powerful fears of being happy, being independent, etc. and often each of those must be accessed and neutralized or eliminated. Underlying all of this is may be the individual's sense that to change means death, even though they are desperately hungry to change!

Usually, we move first to the Narcissistic Parenting aspects, then to the Double Bind aspects and note how smoothly the individual moves through this material. If there is any discomfort the source is accessed and resolved. It is important to manifest the shifts in the Core Beliefs as smoothly and comfortably as possible.

Thirdly, we then symbolically work with the peri-natal material. The Non-Conscious Mind accessing, and creating symbols that represent the feelings and emotions taken on during each of three periods between conception and shortly after birth. Again, any discomfort (Cognitive Dissonance) or block is considered, accessed and resolved.

It is common for individuals to have Core Beliefs about having to restrict their feelings, being dependent, etc. that come forward at unpredictable periods during the course of therapy. When they arise is the time to access and correct them.

Practical Aspects of Therapy

While the foregoing is the most commonly encountered ways and means, other individuals may encounter a different order. For example:

The Double Bind factor may be so prominent in the individual's life that it is quite obvious we should start there. Another individual may reveal obvious patterns of "miserable feelings" that s/he seems to have had "all my life." This may be an indication to start with the peri-natal material first.

The key factor is to start slowly and gently in what seems to be the most obvious arena and go from there. An individual may be quite aware that any time s/he is happy it is followed by anxiety. While it is tempting to begin there, it is usually more effective to access and re-educate one or more of the Limiting Triad legs first. This way the individual has been somewhat strengthened and then dealing with what emotions are permissible is easier and more effective.

A Lifetime of Frustration

We often see individuals who feel there is no hope for them. That whatever they have attempted has never worked for very long, or perhaps seemed to make things worse. As the reader may realize, this is because the very structure of what they are doing to survive means they must limit themselves. Consequently, anything which even feels like the therapeutic approach might eventually be successful, will be avoided at some point.

Fear of Being Successful In Therapy

They run out of money, they get sick, they have car problems, etc. Any individual with any aspect of the Triad should be informed that whatever is being done in the first few hours should be viewed as an experiment. It might seem like it is working, it might not at first. Reminding them during the consultation, and at the beginning of each of the first few sessions, tends to inactivate the fear of success, until it can be accessed and dealt with as it comes up working with the Triad.

Chapter Fourteen

The Re-Defining Process

This chapter describes the approach the authors use to help individuals to "unfold" out of the Triad and other limiting Core Beliefs. As previously indicated, this is accomplished by re-defining the active, life limiting Core Beliefs. It is not the only approach possible, there are many others. The important thing is that you pick someone to help you that you feel confident with and who has a "track record" of being able to help individuals in these problem areas. What follows is the discussion we have with every individual describing how the authors work and the general concepts and procedures that are used.

The Potential Releasing Process

Our Entelechy is the active use of our potential. Every living creature has within it the innate drive to become the highest and finest it is capable of. The more of our potential available for use, the higher and finer the levels of our Entelechy. How much of our potential is available to us at any time, is controlled by our Core Beliefs. These are strongly held beliefs that define us, often occurring in the form of Word Definitions, Laws of Life and Rules of Conduct. They are the controllers of everything we think, say, feel and do. They also directly underlie the physiology of our bodies, state of health and all other areas as well. Core Beliefs may or may not be the same as our conscious beliefs and they may or may not be life enhancing. Whatever they are, they are as powerful in directing us as the lines of code in a computer program are to the computer's function.

The Potential Releasing Process (PReP) has been specially designed to enable you to activate more of your potential and release more of your entelechy in a gentle, effective efficient manner.

"WHAT YOU REALLY BELIEVE IS WHAT YOU GET."

Logical (Conscious or Rational) Mind and Non-Conscious Mind

Let us take a moment to give you a simple, practical concept of how our minds (not the brain—the mind) work:

Logical Mind

The mind which evaluates and sets the goals. How can you tell when you are using this portion of your mind? If someone asks for your name and your thoughts go like this: "Well, let me see, my mother calls me 'Joe', my birth certificate says my name is 'Joe,' my high school diploma says my name is 'Joe,' therefore my name is Joe!" In other words, when you go through a logical line of reasoning to reach the answer, you are using the Conscious mind. Please be aware, that at least for our purposes, the Conscious Mind has only two functions it excels at:

1. to evaluate
2. to set goals

Non-Conscious Mind

This aspect of the mind contains all the other functions of your mind. It includes the automatic control of parts of your body, it creates our dreams, it contains within it your intuition, and it has complete access to everything stored in your memory. It also includes all other aspects of consciousness that it is connected to, such as spiritual. It also has a very important capability of not only being effective within time and space ("local"), but is also not limited "locally," and works outside of time and space ("non-local").

This is extremely important because it can be used to create symbols, answer questions and solve problems while accessing the important information anywhere in time and space. Just what is the Non-Conscious Mind? It has been given many names by many cultures, religions, scientists and philosophers such as:

1. Super Conscious
2. Sub-Conscious
3. Higher Self
4. Higher Consciousness
5. Soul
6. Divine Wisdom
7. Divine Spirit
8. Holy Spirit
9. Shechina
10. Implicate
11. Unconscious
12. God Consciousness
13. Christ Consciousness
14. Spiritual Guide
15. Inner Healer
16. Supreme Consciousness
17. Angelic Self
18. Divine Light
19. God/Goddess Within
20. God Self
21. Inner Teacher
22. Master Teacher
23. Sacred Self
24. Higher Wisdom

25. Inner Divine Wisdom
26. Divine Principle
27. Universal Consciousness
28. Inner Temple
29. Inner Light
30. Morphological Field. (It has recently been suggested that another aspect of the Non-Conscious Mind is an energy field which tells the DNA in each cell what kind of a cell it is to become. Such as: is it to be part of a toe or liver or an eye. This is a kind of energy blueprint and while still a theory, it explains of a lot of phenomena that we have no other satisfactory explanation for. If you are further interested in this Dr. Rupert Sheldrake wrote a vry informative book describing this concept.[50]

If someone asks for your name and you are using your Non-Conscious Mind, the process goes like this:

Q. "What is your name?"
A. "My name is Joe."
In other words, the answer simply pops into mind without you having to do any thinking about it at all.

Logical Mind and Non-Conscious Mind Interaction

You are sitting watching TV. Becoming thirsty, you get up and get a glass of water, however, your mind is still partially involved with the TV program.

Logical Mind has evaluated that you are thirsty and you need to get some water. If it was to continue as a problem solver you would consciously consider every action in order: First I must lean forward, now push myself up, stand on right leg, now stand on left leg, etc. In using the Logical

---

[50] Sheldrake, R. *A New Science of Life*, Tarcher, Houghton, Mifflin Co.1981, ISBN 0-87477-221-4

Mind as a problems solver everything must be worked out in order. Nothing is automatic.

However, Non-Conscious Mind takes over spontaneously once you decide logically to go get a drink. All of the process of standing up, walking to the kitchen, etc., is performed automatically and perfectly. So perfectly that your Logical Mind can be thinking about the program and barely aware that you are walking, getting a glass, filling it with water, etc.

When your Non-Conscious Mind creates a symbol, the symbol simply "pops" into your Logical Mind's awareness without any thinking having occurred. It just suddenly is there.

Suppose you want to go from New York to San Diego. Your Logical Mind has assessed the situation and set the goal of going to San Diego. It then reports this to the Non-Conscious Mind.

If the Non-Conscious Mind was not interfered with, it would take you easily and effortlessly to San Diego. However, the Non-Conscious Mind must first consult with all of your Core Beliefs involved in such a journey. You might think of the Core Beliefs as a Rule Book or set of Automatic Decisions your Logical Mind has developed over many years. These Core Beliefs entail what you really believe about you and your world.

When you put a Core Belief into that Rule Book it is always meant to help – even though years later it may be causing you great problems.

When a Core Belief is operant, that is, when it is active, you feel and act the same way you did when you first took it on.

Consequently you may find yourself acting and feeling in ways that are detrimental to you as an adult and are more like a 2 year old.

Each Core Belief is rooted in at least one Reference Memory. A Reference Memory is one that "proves" the Core Belief is true and accurate.

Since no memory is 100% accurate, that creates a problem in itself. Too, the younger you are when you take on a memory, the more distorted it is AND the more traumatic the event that is put into memory – the more distorted it is. So if it is a very upsetting event and you are very young, the memory that seems so accurate is actually greatly distorted in some ways.

Consider the scenario of going from New York to San Diego. The Non-Conscious Mind checks out all the Core Beliefs about leaving New York, reasons for going, journeying across country by what means and reaching San Diego, being in San Diego, etc…i.e.:

1. If the "bottom line" of your Core Beliefs says it is okay to do all that, you arrive accordingly.
2. If the "bottom line" of your Core Beliefs is that you don't deserve to go to San Diego, then no matter how carefully you plan, you somehow never get there.
3. If the "bottom line" of your Core Beliefs is that you have to go by way of Mexico to get there, then every time you successfully go to San Diego, there will always be some "important" reason to go to Mexico first.

The Pattern always demonstrates the operant Core Beliefs and, of course, we always use our history of the Pattern to prove our Core Beliefs are correct.

These Core Beliefs result in our past being prologue to our future. Also called "self-fulfilling prophecy."

Correction

Consequently, correction involves re-defining the limiting Core Beliefs. This involves either an upgrading or elimination the Core Beliefs involved. And, on occasion, upgrading or re-interpreting the Reference Memories involved.

PReP

PReP is a re-educational process designed to access life limiting Core Beliefs and re-define or eliminate them in order to enable our Core Beliefs to release more of what we are capable of being and doing in life enhancing ways.

The individual is considered a perfect reference book on himself. As that reference book, the individual knows exactly what is going on and how come. S/he may not be consciously aware of that information, but it is always there.

The Entelechist is "stupid" about the individual and has no pre-conceived ideas regarding how the individual should be. The individual makes those final decisions and the Entelechist's role is to help the individual achieve such.

Similarity to Other Approaches

It is similar to some forms of psycho-therapy, however no diagnosis is made nor required.

It is similar to Jungian techniques in that it utilizes symbols; however, it is quite different in that the symbols rarely resemble archetypes. Too, the symbols are spontaneously created by the Non-Conscious Mind, not given by the Entelechist.

It is similar to Adlerian Therapy in that there is special focus at times to the family interaction, but utilizes more psychologically comfortable techniques.

It is similar to hypnosis, relaxation techniques and guided imagery in that other states of consciousness are utilized. It is similar to Cognitive Therapy in that the individual makes new logical decisions, but much of the work is re-educational on quite subtle levels. With PreP most of the new decisions are instigated by the Non-Conscious Mind.

And finally, the spontaneous appearance of the symbols, always reveal the current completeness of the re-educational process.

The Use of Symbols

It has been known for many years that symbols play an important part in our lives. For example, the words you are reading on these pages are actually symbols that your mind automatically converts into messages depending on how the various lines are formed within each symbol (each word).

In some instances symbols are deliberately created by the Logical Mind, such as the logo of a particular corporation or the flag of a country.

In therapeutic settings, the mind is either asked to follow guided imagery (the images being the symbols) or to create its own symbols. Jung described archetypal symbols that seemed to be universal for many cultures. Psycho-synthesis, and other guided imagery techniques, supplied the symbols to the individual, and ask that s/he report what his mind did as each symbol was encountered in a more relaxed, comfortable state—what we call ASC—another state of consciousness. We later discovered that A Superior State of Mind occurred when we asked the Logical Mind to simply be an observer! In our work in Entelechy, we have found, while working with over 3600 individuals, that having that part of the mind which is NOT the logical mind, create the symbol, is much more informative and powerful in aiding individuals to make various shifts in their day to day lives.

Creating Symbols

This is the process we want to occur when we ask your mind to create a symbol about some subject. Your Non-conscious Mind creates the symbol and if it so chooses, presents it to your Logical Mind to see or somehow get in touch with. Your Logical Mind is simply an observer waiting quietly to see what occurs. It does not actively do anything about trying to create the symbol and it does not do anything about trying to change the symbol. It just observes, so if asked, it can report what it saw. If it saw anything.

This is because the Logical Mind is the evaluator, the assessor. It is not the problem solver.

So as you listen to each set of suggestions, please always be aware and understand that it is directed at your Non-Conscious Mind only. You may be fully aware as to what the is being suggested, but <u>all questions, directions and requests are meant to be taken care of by your Non-Conscious Mind only</u>.

This is because the Non-Conscious Mind is the problem solver. It may become an evaluator if so requested by the Logical Mind, but again, it is being a problem solver in doing that assessing.

The Non-Conscious Mind's Symbols

The Non-Conscious Mind is asked to look at the problem in your life that you want to eliminate or correct.

1. It is asked to create a "temporary mental storage area and not show it to the Logical Mind.
2. It then accesses all the Core Beliefs that are causing it to bring into and keep in your life that problem and puts them into that storage area. And, to not show that to the Logical Mind.
3. It then accesses all the reference memories from whichthese Core Beliefs arise. These are the memories, conscious or unconscious, that are the source of these beliefs. It puts them into the mental storage area. And does not show any of this to the Logical Mind.
4. It then traces back into the reference memory of each of the events that first caused you to take on such Core Beliefs.

5. It then accesses the reference memory of each of the events that contributed to you taking on such Core Beliefs.
6. It then accesses the reference memory of each of the events that caused such Core Beliefs that maintain that problem or undesirable pattern in your life to day.
7. It then creates a very abstract symbol, much like a hard to interpret dream, or a weird abstract painting like a Picasso. It may choose to show this to the Logical Mind, if it deems it of value to do so. Otherwise, it is not to reveal the symbol. This symbol has within it all of the following information:

A. All the reference memories involved:

*the core events causing the problem
*the core events contributing to the problem
*the core events maintaining the problem

B. All the Core Beliefs involved:

*The Core Beliefs taken on during each of the core events that are causing the problem.
*The Core Beliefs taken on during each of the core events that contribute to the problem.
*The Core Beliefs taken on during each of the core events maintaining the problem.

Consequently, once the Symbol has been created, any change in this symbol automatically changes the Core Beliefs and the reference memories that are symbolized by that particular part of the Symbol. This must result in a corresponding improvement in your day to day life.

Re-Defining: Upgrading and Correcting

The Logical Mind has no part in evaluating and upgrading the Symbol. In fact, the Non-Conscious Mind often chooses not to show the symbol to the Logical Mind.

Only the Non-Conscious Mind is involved in evaluating, deciding and correcting the Symbol. The Logical Mind has no part in the process. In fact it is discouraged from doing any thing more than simply being an observer.

The Logical Mind does not understand the Symbol (through it may think it does). It does not have all the information as to the reference memories and the Core Beliefs involved and it does not understand the thinking of the Non-Conscious Mind when the Non-Conscious Mind constructed the Symbol! Any changes or modifications made in the Non-Conscious Mind's Symbol automatically changes or modifies either the Core Beliefs involved or the reference memories involved or both. When the Non-Conscious Mind upgrades and improves the Symbol, such upgrades and improvements occur spontaneously. The Logical Mind may actually see this happening or it may see nothing at all happening. In fact, it may not even see the Symbol, for the Non-Conscious Mind has the choice as to whether or not it will even show it to the Logical Mind.

When the reference memories are modified and or the Core Beliefs modified, there is an automatic shift or upgrade in that area in your day to day life.

Basic Areas Covered:
A. The Limiting Triad:
The Limiting Triad consists of three "legs":

1. Narcissistic parenting, also known as self-centered parent or highly controlling parent.

2. Double Bind. Being raised in an environment where as a child you were put "between a rock and a hard place" by being given conflicting orders and expectations.
3. Highly traumatic event, usually from birth to 6 years of age, as a result of which the child decides he or she cannot "do, be or have" what others can.

In a sense, any one of the Triad causes us to act "unreal" because we have come to believe that it is dangerous to be ourselves. When any aspect of the Triad is encountered, we must focus on it so it is neutralized and or its influence negated.

A. The Instinctoid Needs:

1. Autonomy
2. Physical Survival
3. Safety and Security
4. Acceptance and Belonging
5. Giving and Receiving Love including Sexuality
6. Self Esteem, Self Worth

The Core Beliefs about each of these areas may be accessed in one or both of two ways:

As described above with the Symbol.
Having the Non-Conscious Mind create a symbol and show it to the Logical Mind. Here the Logical Mind simply notes what it sees and watches to see if the symbol spontaneously changes.

The choice as to which of the two approaches to use generally unfolds as we proceed with PReP.

B. Special Arenas:

1. Success and Confidence
2. Spirituality
3. Undesirable Copying of another individual
4. Goal Setting
5. Prosperity
6. Physical Disorders
7. Any other arenas that are troubling you or arise in importance. These may need to be approached separately at another time.

During the visit, the individual is asked to note if they are comfortable or uncomfortable throughout the visit. Cognitive Harmony: The individual goes through the visit, comfortable and peaceful. This is evidence that the Core Beliefs being re-structured have no other Core Beliefs interfering. Cognitive Dissonance: If there is a Core Belief that is so limiting that to go against it during the visit results in physical discomfort. This is because the Core Belief being upgraded "threatens" the functioning of a powerful more basic Core Belief and uncomfortable feelings appear. Earphones too tight, room too warm, indigestion, body aches, need to frequently go to the bathroom, etc. If such occurs, the individual is requested to let us know so we can access and work with the interfering Core Belief immediately. Such uncomfortable feelings are always familiar as the individual has experienced them in the past.

Ex:
Individual is hearing suggestions relating to improving self esteem and begins to feel very restless and very bored. The interfering Core Belief causing such feelings is: "If I think well of myself, others will realize that I don't need help and I will not survive."

In general, we expect each person to leave the office, feeling better. We expect that at some point, every thing in their life improves.

Chapter Fifteen

How to Mess Up Your Kids

Messing up your kids – you must remember that kids want to give and receive unconditional love as long as they can. So you just can't do the following once or twice, you have to be consistent.

1. Be consistently erratic, it will drive them crazy trying to figure out what you want them to do, be, have or feel.
2. Don't let your child make any decisions that disagree with yours.
3. Don't let your child have any feelings you can't control. "Pooh-pooh" any of the child's feelings that make you uncomfortable.
4. Tell your child what s/he is really feeling. After all they are just children, how would they know what they really feel.
5. Always give them two distinct opposing commands and then one day one will be right and the next day the other one will be right.
6. It is dangerous to let your children figure you out, after all they might get a sense of what you are really thinking.
7. Always make sure you tell them the opposite of what their other parent has told them. You're the only one that knows what's best for them.
8. Make sure your children appreciate you and all you have done for them, the least they could do is help you out instead of playing some silly games with other kids.
9. If you show them too much love, they'll be spoiled. Don't pick them up. Don't hug them. Don't compliment them.

10. Make sure you pick out what foods they are to eat and how much of each. It doesn't matter what their choices are, you are the parent and you know best.

11. It is probably not wise to allow their friends to come around to the house. It distracts them from doing the chores you have set for them to do.

12. Tell them how wonderful they are one day and how horrible they are the next day. It really sinks in if they are also terrified of you.

13. Always treat them as though you care when the neighbors are watching, but avoid that when there are no neighbors around or the kids will expect you to do that all the time.

14. Always compare them unfavorably to others, it is especially helpful if you pick something different each time so they never get a feeling they have done something right.

15. Depending on whatever mood you are in punish them one day for something you told them was okay the day before.

16. Always be sure to give them a double message such as "Do as I say, not as I do." The really great part of this is that you don't even have to say it out loud, just expect them to know.

17. Be sure to punish them for copying you in various ways, after all, you know you did wrong – sort of, but it is not right for them to do that.

18. Never miss an opportunity to make the child feel guilty. It is a great manipulator to get them to do what you want. Use a lot of "shoulda's" and "coulda's" and "Why didn't you...?" Such as: 'You shoulda known better!"

19. They're kids, you don't really have to listen to them or pay attention when they are trying to talk to you. Make sure you interrupt a lot or walk away or just shrug off

what they are saying when they really need you to just listen.

20. Give a lot of unnecessary and confusing advice.
21. However, always let them know you know best. You have all the answers and they should realize that you are never wrong.
22. Don't ever let them know they have made a good decision and that you trust them to do the right thing, that may make them too independent and you could lose control.
23. When other people are around, talk over the child's head as though s/he isn't there. They should be invisible anyway.
24. Always take out your upsets, frustrations and angers on the kid, when you are really upset about something else. They aren't strong enough to do you any harm if they fight back.
25. If you are playing a game with them, make sure you always win, even if you have to cheat. Its only a kid anyway.
26. Never admit you are wrong, even if you are caught "red-handed."
27. Slap everybody in the house around every now and then. Blame it on being drunk, or something.
28. If the child shows sadness, pain, tears, etc. give it a good shaking and tell it you'll really give it something to be unhappy about.
29. When you spank the child tell it you are only doing it because you love them.
30. Always blame the child for your life/marriage/health/career failing. Especially if they look like someone you hate such as their father, or your ex.
31. When you spank the child, tell it to take the pain as long as it can because that will build toughness.

32. Treat the child who looks like your ex as nasty as you treated your ex.
33. Never say you are sorry to some kid, they'll think they can manipulate you.
34. Compete with the child for your mate's love and attention. Remember all's fair in love and war.
35. Remember your kids are your property; if they develop an identity of their own you will lose your property.
36. If your kids are having a fun time, be sure to step right in and bring an end to that nonsense. If you are not happy, why should they be. Tell them its because:

    a. You have things for them to do.
    b. You don't feel good.
    c. They're making too much noise.

37. Take the older child shopping, buy much of what it wants, let it get really happy and excited and when you get in the car, ask the child when can they pay you back. The parent who consciously and unconsciously finds himself or herself doing any one or a combination of the above, was probably raised the same way. If you are one of those parents, your answer to the questionnaire at the beginning of this book will give you some indication as to where your problems lie.

Chapter Sixteen

Prevention

What Parents Can Do to Prevent

If you do nothing else, show your child love consistently and *in ways that the child will interpret as love*. This is usually sincere physical and verbal expressions of love. Very few children are able to accept that being fed and clothed, etc. means they are loved. The child comes into being internally knowing that love is more than that. If you can't do that, at least do not sabotage the actions of someone else in the family who can. Sincerely praise the child at every chance you get.

Praise [51]

Please note that every statement is followed by an exclamation mark! This is because each of these statements is most effective when expressed with the appropriate energy and feeling. Mumbling it while you walk away makes it a disaster!

INCREDIBLE!
COOL!
GREAT!
AMAZING!
WONDERFUL!

---

[51] POSITIVE PROMOTIONS, 40-01 168th Street Flushing, NY 11358 Phone: 1-800-635-2666 Fax: 1-800-635-2329. (This list may be ordered, in color, on a card.)

HEY! GREAT!
SUPERB!
FAR OUT! A REALLY GREAT PERFORMANCE!
YOU'RE A GOOD FRIEND!
EXCELLENT!
YOU'RE SPECIAL!
YOU'RE A REAL TROOPER!
YOUR WORK IS OUT OF SIGHT!
MARVELOUS!
YOU CAME THROUGH!
YOU TRIED HARD!
YOUR HELP COUNTS!
TERRIFIC!
YOU MADE IT HAPPEN!
FANTASTIC WORK!
FABULOUS!
YOU CAN BE PROUD OF YOURSELF!
KEEP UP THE GOOD WORK!
I KNEW YOU HAD IT IN YOU!
DYNAMITE!
IT'S EVERYTHING I HOPED FOR!
WHAT AN IMAGINATION!
YOU MADE THE DIFFERENCE!
WELL DONE!
VERY GOOD!
FIRST CLASS WORK!
EXCEPTIONAL!
AWESOME!
SUPER JOB!
GOOD FOR YOU!
GREAT ANSWER!
YOU'RE DOING A LOT BETTER!
THANKS FOR BEING HONEST!
YOU'RE A JOY!
HOW ARTISTIC!
HOW THOUGHTFUL OF YOU!

WHAT A GREAT IDEA!
YOU DESERVE A HUG!
YOU'RE GETTING BETTER!
YOU'RE TOPS!
YOU'VE MADE PROGRESS!
YOU'VE GOT WHAT IT TAKES!
YOU'RE #1!
YOU'RE A SHINING STAR!
YOU CAN BE TRUSTED!
YOU'RE A WINNER!
YOU'VE REALLY GROWN UP!
YOU'VE EARNED MY RESPECT!
YOU'RE A GREAT KID!
YOU'RE A CHAMP!
YOU'RE A PLEASURE TO KNOW!
YOU'RE VERY TALENTED!
YOU'RE THE GREATEST!

Isn't it interesting how a few words can strengthen and inspire a child to be more of what it is capable of being? And be so, joyfully. Imagine what would have happened in your life if you had been treated this way!

It appears that the basic cause of depression, rage and limitation in children and adults lies in the teaching of the child to not be "real." That is: to not be who and what s/he is. Thus, the preventative "treatment" is to encourage the child to be a happy, unique, curious, expressive individual who has choices and who is taught to accept responsibility for the choices s/he makes. Parental figures do not usually deliberately raise children to live in fear, guilt and tension. We say "not usually" as some parents are quite specific about this. The children of the son of a German immigrant were quickly taught that his word was law; that his needs came first. That they were to be seen and not heard. And, for amusement he would confuse them about the money he said he would pay them for doing chores.

Because of his erratic and deliberate behavior, the children were constantly upset and Thus constantly unwilling to reveal themselves because he would deliberately attack them. Children need to have clear cut boundaries and limits that are fair and reasonable. They also need to have clear cut penalties for exceeding those boundaries and limits.

What Parents Can Do to Undo Present Situation

The problem here is that the narcissistic parent functions with a set of blinders on. If you were to point out to such a parent what s/he is doing to his/her child, you would be met with a variety of defenses designed to prevent changing the circumstances.

The narcissistic parent most often feels like a failure; inadequate, insecure, incapable, depressed, helpless and powerless. The narcissistic parent, expects the child to do for the parent what the parent could not do. Or a narcissistic parental figure may take out on the child anything which seems to make the child more than the parent. Rather intensive therapeutic intervention is required to help such a parent shift out of such behavior towards their child.

Aside from that, anything which helps the child to understand and realize that they have a right to whatever they are feeling, and that such feelings are valid and worth listening to, is a start in the right direction. The child should be encouraged to communicate exactly what they are thinking and feeling without fear of retribution. The child should be encouraged to set its own goals and be responsible for its decisions. Mistakes should be used as teaching experiences rather than to bring down punishment.

Establishing Self Esteem [52]

Share your experiences, ideas and future goals with your child.

Encourage your child to look within for choices or decisions.

Love your child unconditionally and accept any shortcomings as part of being human.

You may not approve of what the child did, but this should not stop your love of your child.

Focus on your child's educational progress and feelings about school. Listen to your child's ideas and concerns.

Enter into a partnership with your child's school to insure the best education for your child.

involve your child in the daily decision-making process; ask his or her opinion to encourage a sense of responsibility and belonging. No matter how ridiculous the child's ideas may seem, consider them seriously without deprecating the child or hurting its feelings.

Give your child choices as much as possible.

Part of childhood is making mistakes and learning from them.

Encourage your child to be expressive and to always communicate in a non-threatening manner.

Make sure you know your child's friends and families; if necessary, be the parent to set values such as respect and cooperation.

If you, as a parent, cannot do these things, then we strongly urge you to get professional help. Whatever is preventing you from being the kind of parent your child needs, is also causing

52 Ibid (This list, too, may be ordered in color on a card from Promotions.) great turmoil in your life, whether you are consciously aware of it or not.

About the Authors

Joseph E. Spear, D.O. was born September 17, 1930 in Oneonta New York. He received his degree from Philadelphia College of Osteopathy in 1957. He went on to intern at Bayview Hospital in Bay Village, OH.

Cecelia Ann Spear, M.A. received her Masters degree in Psychological Counseling. The authors have been collaborating on this work since they began working on this project, Entelechial Therapy, since 1967. They were married in December of 1972. Their family currently includes six children, four grandchildren, and one great-grand child.